INSTAGRAM MARKETING BLUEPRINT 2021

THE PRACTICAL GUIDE& SECRETS FOR GAINING
FOLLOWERS, BECOMING AN INFLUENCER,
BUILDING A PERSONAL BRAND & BUSINESS &
MASTERING SOCIAL MEDIA ADVERTISING

BRANDON'S BUSINESS GUIDES

CONTENTS

INTRODUCTION

Most people associate Instagram with luxurious photos and cute animals. When I think of Instagram, I see an untapped opportunity - a gold mine that anyone can leverage to gain fame, influence, and success. If you've picked up this book intending to become an Instagram influencer, a social media marketer, or to grow your brand, then you're in the right place.

While Instagram is a top-rated social media platform for smartphone addicts, it has also proven to be an excellent investment for savvy marketers and business owners. It took a while for me to realize this. Once it dawned on me that I could grow my business even more by leveraging this platform, I made the decision to study, experiment with, and build my brand on the platform. So far, it has yielded outstanding results. My guess is that you picked up this book because you're looking to do something similar, either for a personal or business brand. Maybe it's not even your brand you want to help build. Both employees and entrepreneurs can benefit from the strategies contained in this Instagram playbook.

The intention here is to share all the secrets I've learned so that you can avoid making some of the mistakes newer marketers are making. Mistakes I made when I set up my account.

Instagram has so much potential, but it requires a good plan. You need to know the right steps to follow to go from an average account posting pretty pictures randomly to an epic business account that generates revenue.

Unfortunately, there's a lot of misinformation and over-whelm around the topic of Instagram marketing. When you're just starting out, it's hard to know what those initial steps should be and where you ought to focus your time, energy, and resources.

If you attempt to copy mega influencers who have already invested over a decade on the platform, you will fail badly. The other thing to note is that your ambition and desire to grow a following fast is noble, but it won't happen in the first month you launch. By going through this book and implementing all that you'll learn, your following will grow, but your focus must shift from acquiring a large following to attracting an audience that resonates and connects with what you have to offer. A mistake many people make is to focus on getting that blue tick or becoming mega-influencers. That's the wrong approach.

The best way to succeed on Instagram is to focus on establishing yourself as someone worth following. You need to build your reputation and give people the chance to see that you're authentic, trustworthy and that you care about your tribe.

If you consider that over 62% of Instagram users say they've become more interested in a brand or product after seeing it in Stories and at least 80% of users follow a business, I'd say it's vital to establish your brand the right way.

So, let's start by eliminating some of the common mistakes that usually cause brands to fail on the platform.

#1: Avoid starting your Instagram journey without a clear goal and strategy in place.

This should be Instagram 101, yet most influencers and start-ups often skip over it. If you don't start with a strategy, you have no solid foundation. Without clear goals, targets, and a plan, you might end up wasting opportunities, losing morale because you don't see traction fast enough, and like most people, you'll conclude that Instagram doesn't work.

Don't worry if you're already frazzled about strategy because this playbook gives you a walkthrough of how to create one now.

#2: Avoid using a personal and private account.

By having a private account or a personal account, you will not have access to many of the wonderful features that Instagram offers. You'll also lose followers because most new followers steer clear of an Instagram profile with the "Private" icon.

#3. Focusing on quantity instead of quality is another mistake that must be avoided at all costs.

You'll find lots of reminders throughout this book that emphasize the importance of quality and serving your audience. That is by design. You see, after hustling on Instagram for a few years, I finally started generating income from my efforts. I can recall the first time I made $10,000 in a single month from my Instagram campaign. The shift I had made a few months earlier was pretty simple, yet it led to this tremendous income growth. What was the change? I stopped focusing on how merely posting for the sake of volume and wholly discarded the idea of buying followers so my account could look like it had a huge following. Instead, I focused all my energy on producing helpful and inspiring content.

Now, this doesn't mean you can't post several times a day. What I want you to realize is that quality should never be compromised for the sake of quantity.

#4: Avoid the temptation of buying followers.

I must admit when starting from zero, this option does sound appealing for any ambitious entrepreneur or influencer. I almost fell for it as well. But after observing how some of my friends were growing after purchasing thousands of followers for a few bucks, I realized it wasn't an approach that suited me. Ultimately this will have to be a personal decision. I believe that getting real followers who love your content is worth a lot more than any perception millions of bought followers could give your account.

#5: Do not misuse hashtags. It will mess with your brand credibility and stunt your growth. The last thing I want to mention before we jump into the first section of this playbook is that hashtags are valuable. Treat them with respect. Be strategic about which hashtags you choose to use. Don't just spam your content with trending hashtags because some guru said you could get free traffic. Although Instagram allows up to 30 hashtags per post, please don't fill up your captions and obscure your brand's vision with too many hashtags.

We will talk more about this in a later chapter. For now, I want you to understand that Instagram is a platform that works best when authenticity and quality take the lead, so choose your hashtags wisely.

Most people assume all it takes to succeed on Instagram is to post attractive images, but the fact is, this is a serious business. You should treat Instagram as a real business if you want it to give you a good investment return. So, before we get started, let's make each other a promise. If you commit to this journey and treat Instagram marketing with the same level of dedication and persistence that you would any business development project, I promise to give you all the tools, hacks, and strategies you need to succeed.

SECTION 01: UNDERSTANDING INSTAGRAM

WHAT YOU NEED TO KNOW BEFORE GETTING STARTED

Instagram stands at over 1 billion monthly users, and over 500 million people are using Instagram Stories daily. Did you know that? I mean, those are huge numbers for a simple image-sharing social network. The best part is, you can find both a male and female audience hanging out on Instagram, so whether you're serving a small niche of men or a sizeable stay-at-home mom audience, you can generate healthy attention on this platform. If those facts haven't yet excited you, here are some recent statistics about Instagram for business and user behavior.

- A third of the most viewed Stories on Instagram are from businesses.
- At least 63% of Instagram users login to the

platform once per day, and 42% do it multiple times. That means, as long as you know your audience and the best times to post, your content can receive really great engagement.

- 200 million Instagram users say they visit at least one business profile daily. By setting up your profile the right you, your business might be the one they visit next.

- For brands looking to serve the U.S audience, Instagram is a goldmine, with 11% of American users reporting that their top reason for using the platform is to shop or find new products. The buyer cycle tends to be earlier in the purchase journey, so keep that in mind as you plan your campaigns.

- U.S marketers love spending their budget on influencer marketing, especially on this platform. 69% have a budget to invest in Instagram influencers. That's a larger figure than YouTube influencer marketing opportunities.

- Brands pay (on average) between $100 - $2,085 for influencers to post on the feed or Instagram Stories. So, if you're an influencer, get excited because we'll talk more about this income-earning opportunity.

If you are starting to see the opportunity at hand, then I'm glad. Instagram and social media at large could be the missing key to unlocking your dream lifestyle. Before you roll up your sleeves and start mining for the gold that awaits you, I'd like to give you an overview of the power of social media and why it is such a powerful vehicle for sales and marketing.

A better understanding of social media

To understand social media and win on Instagram, you need to understand human psychology. We are social creatures. It is in our DNA to come together, share, exchange, and build connections through social gatherings. Modern science has proven the importance and benefit both mentally and physically for encouraging social connections. Since the advent of the Internet, we have taken this innate desire that's been going on since our years as cave people and turned into a daily habit that takes place via technology and our smartphones. Social media platforms aren't just trendy; they have become a new way of life.

Thanks to social media, we can meet new people, keep in touch with friends and family living far and near. We can connect with like-minded individuals who share the same values and beliefs we have regardless of location. We can freely express our opinions about any topic (just recall how crazy the last U.S presidential elections were on the Internet, and you'll understand the power of social media). I could continue naming how impactful social media is in our modern world, but I think you get it. The best part is that businesses of all sizes, including startups, have realized this truth too. Savvy entrepreneurs have entered the scene across the major social networks, including YouTube, Facebook, Instagram, Twitter, LinkedIn, and others intending to leverage these platforms.

Never has it been easier for a self-made individual in any industry to build a brand, share a message, and impact the lives of millions of people. And you have the power to do it too, regardless of budget, experience, age, ethnicity, or location. What I love about social media is that you have in your hand the power to impact others, express your authentic truth, and make some good money in the process.

The journey and history of social media has been long. On the resource page, I have listed an article that might be an exciting read for those interested in learning the early years of social media as a whole.

Our focus is on Instagram in this book, but I encourage you to get some of my other books, such as the YouTube Playbook if you want to master more than one social media platform.

THE HISTORY AND GROWTH OF INSTAGRAM

Selfies have become an obsessive and addictive behavior in our society, but who can blame these half-naked boys and girls who like to show off their perfect images on Instagram? I mean, after all, we have always had a soft spot for pictures. Even before we became civilized, we were drawing paintings on the walls. So clearly, visual elements are very appealing to us. Before October 2010, when Instagram was launched, sharing pictures was quite cumbersome. Instagram came into the scene to change how we connect and share through visual content. By 2012, Facebook took the leap and bought the image-sharing app, and since then, it has been growing in both popularity and style.

The founders of Instagram intended to create an app that would create a connection and cheer people up. So, for example, if you had a friend on the other side of the world freezing in the cold of winter and dreaming of a beautiful summer sunset, you could take a snapshot of your environment and instantly send it to your friend. Kevin Systrom was the guy who started working on what would become Instagram as we know it today. Kevin had no formal training but learned how to code during his spare time (weekends and after work). After meeting Mike Kreiger, the side project turned into Instagram.

The first attempt was made solely by Systrom as called Burbn, which didn't succeed as he had hoped. By the time Kreiger came on board, Burbn was being used mainly to share photos. People loved sharing coffee pics, dog pics, bathroom selfies, and so on. After much research, they decided to transform Burbn into Scotch (true story! And yes, they obviously enjoyed naming their projects after alcohol). Unfortunately, scotch was full of bugs, and the after-taste effects weren't that pleasant, so the founders kept tinkering until Instagram was finally launched in October of 2010. That first day of launch, the Instagram app had twenty-five thousand users and growing.

Within three months, they hit one million users and the rest, as they say, is success history since, as you know, Mark Zuckerberg bought Instagram for $1 billion in April 2012.

The fascinating thing about Instagram is that its simplicity and ability to make an ordinary picture look extraordinary is the secret sauce behind its success. Lean into this innate desire for attractive visual elements, and you will build a decent audience on Instagram to meet your objectives.

People use Instagram as a place to connect, get inspired, and share their feelings. They've recently started relying on Instagram to connect with new brands and discover new products from their favorite brands. I've also observed that Instagram users love using the app as a way to escape their daily mundane or perhaps stressful realities. That's why you'll find crazy engagement and interaction in particular niches, especially travel. But we will talk more about niches and how to drive engagement in an upcoming chapter.

Now that you understand a bit of Instagram history, user psychology, and the app's intention, let's talk about how it works.

HOW INSTAGRAM WORKS

Instagram is free to set up an account and use. It works on all iPhones, iPads, Android devices, and tablets from Samsung, Google, and others. Although it can be accessed from a desktop or laptop, it is designed to be a mobile app. As I said before, this is one of the most popular social networks, both with teens and adults. You can take a standard pic and do things such as applying filters, adjusting brightness, color overlay, and a few other technical things. You can also create short videos to post either on your Feed, IGTV, or Instagram Stories, which we will discuss at length.

The first step you need to take is to download the app to your smartphone and sign up so you can easily follow along as each chapter unfolds new strategies to implement. Once you've signed up, you will get a personal account, which can later be adjusted to a business or creative account. If you have a Facebook account, I encourage you to link them once you're done with the sign-up. That will enable you to take advantage of the cross-messaging feature that Instagram recently released. You will then need to fill in your bio information, add a profile picture, and customize a few other things that we will delve into in a little while.

Each time you open the app on your phone, you'll automatically refresh your main feed, and the algorithm will populate your screen with content from the accounts you've shown interest in. On the bottom of the app should be a menu bar with the Home, Explore, Reels, Instagram Shop, and Profile tabs to help you navigate your account.

At the top right-hand, you will have access to the camera (camera icon), direct messages (through the messages icon), and activity where you can see likes and comments. Now you can use that same button at the top of the Home tab to create a post, a story, or a reel.

From your personal profile feed, you'll see on the top right-hand corner a plus + sign that allows you to create a post, a story, a story highlight, an IGTV video, a reel, or a guide. There's also a collapsed menu that expands when you click the three parallel bars icon. Here you will find Settings, Archive, Insights, your activity, QR Code, Saved, Close Friends, and Discover people.

Speaking of the algorithm populating your feed, let's share what's known about the Instagram algorithm.

THE INSTAGRAM ALGORITHM

At first, you will be encouraged to follow accounts so that the algorithm can learn what you care about. It will also continue to monitor your activity in the background to figure out what content you're engaging with. In a little while, you will only start to see fresh content from the accounts you most engage with. That is the same experience all users have on the platform. Therefore, what we know for sure based on observation and what the Instagram team has shared is that the algorithm will prioritize which content to show first based on assumed relationship. What do I mean?

An illustration will explain better. Suppose you a friend, and you're always commenting on his or her posts, or they keep tagging you in their content. It's likely you'll always see what they post because Instagram will populate your feed with more of their content. It assumes this engagement implies that you're categorizing this account as "friends and family." Theoretically, the more you interact with an account, even if you hate that account and are posting hate comments, the more you will see their content on your feed.

Now flip this around and think about your audience. The more they interact with and engage with your content whenever you post, the more likely they are to keep seeing your content on their feed. The algorithm uses signals such as:

- Direct messages
- People searched for
- Hashtags used

These activities signal to the algorithm that the user wants to interact more with the account they frequently engage in. Based on that behavior pattern, the algorithm populates the feed with more content from those accounts.

We also know from the Instagram team that, aside from relationships, they focus on timeliness, interest, frequency, usage, and following to determine what content to rank on the user's feed. Let's break down each of these a little more.

- Timeliness - It simply means that Instagram wants to show fresh content. So, something from last week might not show up on a user's feed because it's perceived as outdated. Each time a user logs back into their feed, Instagram wants to show them the latest and best content that was posted since their last visit. Which leads to our next micro-signal.

- Frequency - When it comes to frequency, it's about showing the user as much of the best and most relevant content as possible. The algorithm tries to show the newly logged-in user the best of what they've missed since their last visit. So, if your user logs in daily or even several times a day and you only post once a week, you might end up losing that connection because Instagram won't have anything fresh to show, and that will lead to lower engagement.

- Interest - This implies that the order in which a user will see content on their feed is determined by what the algorithm believes will be of most significant interest to the person. So, the more relevant and interesting a piece of content to a particular user, the higher it will rank on the feed. The algorithm uses photo recognition technologies, hashtags, and the copy on the post to categorize and rank it.

- Following - This implies that the algorithm sorts through all the accounts a user follows to determine what to show him or her when the app is opened. The more accounts a user follows, the higher the competition, of course, because the algorithm can only select a few accounts. It will fall back on the main criteria of relationship, i.e., friends, family, and favorite accounts.

- Usage - The algorithm will monitor the time spent on the app. Some people log in multiple times a day for short periods. Others like to binge-scroll through the feed for long sessions each day. Depending on the particular use case, the algorithm will prioritize and order the content from the highest priority to enhance user experience. Therefore, if your content isn't appealing and relevant enough based on the algorithm's criteria, your content may never show up on your followers' feeds. Therefore, it is of utmost importance to get into this Instagram game with the intention of providing quality content. Your posts must be clear enough for the algorithm to interpret appropriately. They must be targeted to the right audience and interesting enough for the end-user.

How To Leverage The Algorithm And Instagram Features To Grow Your Brand And Business.

By learning how the algorithm prioritizes content, I think you can create an advantage for yourself because you can commit to producing content that you feel confident about. And then, it's up to you to put some effort and creativity so that your followers can engage with you more so that Instagram can categorize your account as a high priority. How do you do this? There are many ways to build that relationship, and you will learn hacks and content types as the book unfolds. A few examples include creating video messages and initiating video calls for your followers. Creating fun Stories and making it interactive by adding a question sticker. You can also share longer edited videos with IGTV. A cool feature that many business owners are using nowadays is the QR code. It's a great way to bridge the online and offline world, especially if you already have an existing offline business. For example, if you're a bakery, someone can come in for some fresh bread, and before leaving you could ask them to scan the QR code that leads to your Instagram Page. Or you can easily send it over as a text either to their number or email address. It's a great way to get more followers, likes, direct messages, and even sales because you can send them promos after they're gone.

Want Your Very Own QR Code?

It used to be that you'd have to create your QR code either from Google or by hiring someone to do it for you. However, an update that just happened recently by Instagram makes your ability to have a QR code super easy. Simply open up your Instagram app and head over to your main profile feed. On the upper right-hand corner, you'll see the menu icon (three parallel lines). Click on that to open up a list of options, including your in-built QR code.

I absolutely love this new feature because you can even customize your QR code's look and background feel by taking a selfie that Instagram automatically attaches. You also can share the QR code right from the app to WhatsApp, Messages, Email, Facebook, LinkedIn, and so much more.

2

WHAT MOTIVATES YOU

*I*nstagram is one of the best social platforms to grow your brand and make sales, even if you're a beginner in online marketing. But let's get something straight, it's still going to be a hustle. You will need to put in a tremendous amount of effort to generate enough momentum for your account. That's why you need to connect with your motive for getting started on this path. If you don't have clarity on why you're doing this and what motivates you, the lack of engagement and growth bound to occur in the early phases of your journey will cause you to give up too soon.

Often you will see reports from small and large brands alike showing how fast they grew on a social network or how crazy their return on investment was for a particular social media campaign. It's easy to assume the same will happen to you. I'm sorry to burst your bubble, but it won't.

You're not going to go from zero to Instagram famous in a few weeks or months. If that's why you picked up this book, then you need to find that kind of "get rich quick" mentality elsewhere. The reality of doing business is that rarely do you have that stroke of luck and experience business miracles. The general rule of thumb is the slow grind and build up to what will eventually become a huge success. So, buckle up and anchor yourself in the thing that motivates you. Some people are motivated by their business goals. Others care about changing their lifestyles or becoming social media influencers. Whatever your "WHY" might be, connect with it and keep yourself grounded in it.

WHY USE INSTAGRAM?

Another question you'll need to answer is why you're choosing to grow your Instagram channel. Why not YouTube or LinkedIn? Give yourself a clear answer to this. I can share with you why I started using Instagram to market my business, and I also have reasons given to me by peers and students of my online courses.

- Instagram is simple and easy to use. Compared to other channels, the simplicity and aesthetics of the platforms are very appealing for end-users. That leads me to my second point.

- Instagram has serious engagement levels. Compared to other channels such as Facebook and Twitter, you can be a brand-new account and still get an audience discovering and liking your content. For a solopreneur or start-up, this kind of organic engagement is priceless.

- Instagram is known for nurturing and launching influencers successfully. Suppose you dream of becoming a social media influencer. In that case, Instagram is one of the best places to build your audience. Brands already know and budget for influencer marketing in 2021, and audiences engage more with influencers they know, like, and trust. Making a lucrative career on Instagram is highly probably even if you're a stay-at-home mom or a struggling artist, and that will lead to tremendous financial freedom.

- Partnering with influencers is easier on Instagram for business owners. The flip side of that influencer marketing concept is that as business owners and thought leaders, we can quickly get our account in front of a new and engaged audience without breaking the bank. There are different levels of influencers, each with their own pricing options.

You could spend zero money, a few hundred dollars or several thousand depending on your budget and the relationships you build. In so doing, your brand, products, or services can be promoted by the said influencer to bring your sales game to a whole other level. More on influencers and influencer marketing later.

- You can make money directly from Instagram. As a business owner, revenue is extremely important to me. Instagram is very appealing because, through product placements, we can add tags to products in our photos with links that include product description, price, and the ability to "shop now." That means a user can go from Instagram to your online store in seconds, leading to sales. The best part is, over seventy percent of users report they enjoy purchasing products through social media. So, what are you waiting for? Start planning how to engage people and drive traffic to your checkout page.

INSTAGRAM GOAL SETTING

If you've spent enough time online or invested in personal development programs, then the idea of goal setting will not be a new concept. Without a target to aim for, it's hard to measure progress or even attain any level of success. Think of it like this... If you get into your car and start driving west, you could be driving forever because "west" could take you anywhere. Eventually, you'll run out of gas, the car will break down, or you'll get tired and give up without any sense of satisfaction.

To experience the level of fulfilment and success we all crave, goal setting is essential in our personal and professional lives. This isn't a session on personal achievement and satisfaction, however, so if you're still confused about why you need goals, I suggest getting a book from a guru like Jack Canfield, Brian Tracy, John Assaraf, or one of those online gurus who teach that stuff. For our Instagram success and brand growth, setting the right goals will enable us to track progress, monitor growth, and determine what works and what doesn't. It will give us a sense of direction and a focusing point, which is essential in the noisy social media world. It will also enable us to discipline ourselves and avoid falling for the shiny object syndrome that usually distracts many social media marketers.

If you have no idea how to set your social media goals, here's something simple you can follow.

First, I want you to determine and align your social media goals with your business goals. For example, your business goal might be to increase brand awareness. In that case, a great social media goal can be to increase organic reach. Coschedule created a fantastic guideline you can use as a reference. For the sake of convenience, I am sharing their basic outline below.

Increase online sales (Business Objective) can align with tracking conversions from social referrals.

Boosting brand loyalty (Business Objective) can align with tracking the number of new subscribers that come from Instagram.

Increase revenue from new products launched (Business Objective) can align with tracking conversions from Product Campaigns from Instagram.

This is, of course, just a guideline if you already have a business.

The second thing you need to do is set your S.M.A.R.T (**S**pecific **M**easurable **A**spirational **R**elevant **T**imely) goals. How do you do this on Instagram? By clearly defining what you want to achieve within a specified timeframe. For example, if you're a personal trainer looking to use Instagram to acquire new clients, then a great S.M.A.R.T goal would be: Convert ten appointments within 30days by posting once a day on Instagram feed and three times a day on Stories with a clear call-to-action. My paid ads budget is $10 per day that runs a campaign leading to my landing page with the "book free session now" button. The more detailed your goal, the better. If you're more interested in growing followers, then your first goal should, of course, reflect that.

The third thing to do here before you complete setting your goals for Instagram is to clarify what kind of a goal you will focus on to meet that overall business objective. Here's why. Marketing is deep. You can either create a campaign for branding or selling, but it's rare that you can hit both properly. Unfortunately, few people understand the difference between branding and selling, so most social media content comes across as spammy.

To help you stand out for all the right reasons, I encourage you to have a healthy mix of branding and selling content on your Instagram feed. Your social media strategy should include both aspects because different people will interact with your account at different points of their buying journey. You need both branding and selling to thrive, so get creative with this.

Since you're at the early stages of the business development on Instagram, you should have a primary business objective with a social media goal that aligns with that objective. Then you should further break down that social media objective into milestones. So, going back to the personal trainer example. He should break down the goal of selling ten appointments further (especially if he's just started building up his

Instagram account) into smaller milestones. Perhaps he can break it down to how many followers he will need and what level of engagement he will be looking for before moving that audience into the phase of asking them to check out his landing page and book a session. Then he would be able to do both branding and conversion goals, all for that same overall objective and getting ten new client appointments.

Remember, branding should be done consistently. It should be focused on giving. Goals for branding include increasing follower count, increasing reach, likes, shares, comments, mentions, DMs, and saves. Most of this happens organically and over a long period of time. It will require daily posts, lots of research, and you figuring out what your audience wants and where they are so you can engage with them and pull them into your world. If, for example, you want to grow your account to 100,000 followers in twelve months, that would be considered a branding goal. There are action steps you need to take to make that happen. On Instagram, we value a lot the level of engagement. The more people comment, reply to Stories with a chat, direct message you, and of course heart your stuff, the more you'll know you're growing.

When it comes to conversions that lead to sales, the best approach, in my opinion, is soft selling. Direct (hard selling) doesn't seem to work on social media, especially Instagram.

People don't want to be sold to. They want to be served. So, for example, instead of the personal trainer focusing on a hard sell asking for people to book a private session, he can post customer success stories with happy clients who've gone through his program successfully. If he targets people looking to lose weight fast, he could post a video with his client, who lost weight in time for her wedding. That will drive more engagement and create awareness around his special program. It subtly suggests to the user that they should click on his bio to access the same magical program if they wish to experience similar results.

Therefore, I encourage you to approach Instagram through this lens of adding value first. Think of growing a community and serving your audience instead of selling your products or services.

If you want to become an Instagram influencer and get brands to pay you lots of money for a shout out, then make sure you establish that credibility as someone who serves and provides exceptional content and value. The actual product you promote and encourage people to buy should be an add-on, not the main reason for creating your content - in the user's eyes. If you can achieve this high level of content creation, conversions and sales will become an easy game on Instagram.

What Are The Common Goals For Influencers And Business Owners On Instagram?

Increasing product sales, raising brand awareness, increasing followers, driving traffic to a landing page or website, customer service, and customer satisfaction. You can also have the goal of list building or identifying and building relationships with key influencers in your niche.

Before your Instagram account can yield desired goals and results, you need to commit. Your ability to consistently show up and put out great content without losing enthusiasm will go a long way toward attaining your desires. So, before we jump into the technicalities of setting up your account and growing it the right way, let's talk about getting your mind right.

STICKING TO WHAT YOU BELIEVE IN

If it's unclear to you at this point, let me emphasize that you determine your growth and success on Instagram. The platform is straightforward, and your ability to communicate your message and attract your audience is pretty standard because it's an open playing field. The difference between you and every other business owner or influencer is the mindset you're operating on. That becomes the determining factor of whether you will rise and succeed or drown and fail. Therefore, getting your mind right is just as important as learning what to post, when to post, and hacks for generating engagement - do you agree?

After being online for over a decade, I realize success, fame, and fortune doesn't just come by luck or accident. There are certain qualities and practices that lead people to their dream lifestyles.

Ever heard of the saying "success leaves clues"? Well, I've been observing and learning from incredibly successful mentors, and I've noticed certain commonalities.

Every successful person I know in the online world possesses a certain mindset, approaches their work in a specific way, and is driven by their WHY. They didn't just jump into social media for the sake of it. Those that are influencers know why they want to become successful social media influencers. Business owners looking to grow successful social media channels have clarity on why this is important to them. I want you to have that same level of clarity.

The other common trait you will find is that all successful individuals only talk about, teach, and promote what they believe in. It's not fake or hyperbole. They don't just accept partnerships or paid gigs for the sake of making a dollar. The best influencers on Instagram are only working with companies, products, and brands they genuinely believe in. The best business owners only post content and share the knowledge they've had experience in and are super passionate about. That leads to my big key takeaway for you. Stick to your truth and only share what you know and believe in.

If the content you create comes from that authentic place of passion, talent, and skill, you will not run dry, despair, or easily fall out of love with content creation because you'll be doing something you care about deeply. And because this is something you would do anyway, the hardships of growing your account won't wear you down. It will be easy to persevere and stick with your channel until your goals are attained. That is the path to success and whatever fame you wish to reap from Instagram. It won't be easy, and it's unlikely to happen overnight. But if you still feel this is your time to become Instagram famous after reading this last section, then move on to the next chapter because you're ready to go big.

SECTION 02: INSTAGRAM ACCOUNT

3

FIRST, YOU NEED A NICHE

Whenever this topic of choosing a niche comes up, I always receive mixed reactions. Some people get it immediately, while others assume, I am suggesting they limit their creativity. There was a time when social media was young and unsaturated with noisemakers that anyone with a good brand and powerful message could stand out immediately. Those days are gone.

Social media is reaching maturity, and when networks like Instagram begin to boast the numbers currently reported (over 1 billion users), it's time to take a different approach. The riches are in the niches. You will struggle to build something substantial on Instagram or any large social network if you don't first figure out your niche.

WHY NICHING DOWN IS SO IMPORTANT.

I bet you're asking yourself why it's important to niche down. It's a great question, and you'll often hear varying answers. Some experts claim niching down is essential because it helps clarify your message and brand identity. That's true. Others will tell you that niching down enables you to quickly establish yourself as an authority in a specific topic, which will grow your following faster. That is also true. For me, the whole concept of niching down has become fundamental because of the shift in user behavior. We have seen a rise, stabilization, and a drop in social media usage in larger networks in recent years. Please don't misunderstand; I am not saying there are no people on Facebook, Twitter, Instagram, and all these big social networks. Data proves that the numbers are still staggering. But despite boasting huge numbers, the drop continues, and users are starting to slow down and even refrain from engaging too much on these large networks. Instead, they seem to prefer smaller and more personalized social gathering spaces where direct contact with like-minded people feels easier. As a result, marketing on social media is taking on a new look, and those that are winning are the business owners and influencers who are focused on a specific niche.

When you niche down, you're not permanently cutting yourself off other areas of interest you might have. Instead, you are laser focusing on a single topic or area of expertise that acts as a beacon for like-minded individuals who care about that same subject. By niching down your odds of standing out, reaching your target audience, and generating higher engagement significantly increase. Whether you're an entrepreneur or influencer, that alone can shave down the journey of becoming successful on Instagram.

Many successful Instagrammers have shared stories of how they got started. Their content was all over the place. They were attempting to succeed by drawing in a broad audience, and it didn't pan out. But after picking a niche and drilling down to that single subject matter, things started shifting as they saw their tribe forming. It makes for a very effective marketing strategy.

Some people will read the first few paragraphs and know immediately what niche to go after. If that's you, congratulations! I struggled for several months before figuring out what could become my niche because I had so many passions and different skills. I had worked in several industries, and I loved business, personal development, DIY, and playing the guitar. As you can imagine, it was tough for me to focus on one niche for Instagram. If you're multi-talented and multi-passionate, then don't worry. You're not alone. This chapter will provide a guideline to help you hone in and narrow down your focus.

INSTAGRAM NICHES

There are thousands of niches on Instagram, and I'm pretty sure the numbers will keep growing. That means whatever niche you choose, there's likely to be a ready-built audience and some competition. Trust me, you want competition, and later on, I will explain why. If you're starting your Instagram account to generate sales, then you want to make sure the niche is profitable. But don't pick a niche just because it's a money-maker! Here are some of the popular niches:

Lifestyle

The lifestyle niche is all about showcasing how incredible and inspiring your life is. It's about sharing your opinions, ideas, and truth. People love listening to amazing stories and envisioning themselves as part of those stories. If you have something that could wow your followers, something that would make people wish they were in your shoes or motivate them to think outside the box, then this niche might be for you.

Food and cooking

Who doesn't love good food? Regardless of how advanced we become as civilized people; food will always be a huge part of our lives. That's why Instagram favors the food niche a lot. Cooking continues to gain popularity on the platform as people share recipes, cooking tips, tutorials, and more. If your love is in food, no matter how unknown your type of cuisine, you can build a tribe around your topic as long as it's good food and great content.

Business

If you love the world of start-ups, small businesses, and entrepreneurship, this might be the niche for you. There are so many business opportunities that can lead to income thanks to the Internet. If money-making is a passion, you could also create an account sharing ideas, tips, and motivation so your followers can make money and gain financial freedom.

Fashion

Fashion niches are booming on Instagram, and with good reason. Brands of all sizes invest a significant amount of money on the platform, and users flock to these alluring accounts where they can get inspired, entertained, and even educated on how they should look. People care about how they look and even more, so they want to know what celebrities are wearing. If you're passionate about fashion or have experience in this industry, this might be worth your time as there is a ready audience waiting to see what you can offer.

Beauty

More popular than fashion on Instagram is beauty. Over 96% of all beauty brands have invested in a strong Instagram presence. I'm guessing it's because many teenagers and women love interacting with beauty products on Instagram. Users want to see tutorials, beauty tips, product reviews, and whatever else you can cook up. Creativity and authenticity are going to be critical here. The more unique your content, the better it will perform.

Health and Fitness

Many people have started prioritizing health and wellbeing, especially since the 2020 pandemic. So, it shouldn't come as a surprise that the health and fitness niche is a profitable option. It can be a subset of fitness or purely focused on nutrition. Regardless of your preference, you have a good chance of growing and monetizing your expertise with a bit of creativity and hard work.

Animals

People on Instagram love pets. Some accounts dedicated to animals (including pets) have become so popular they outshine human celebrities. So, if you're passionate about any type of creature, it's probable that you can grow a decent following and fan base around your non-human friend.

Memes

Instagram is full of memes. They are entertaining, quick to create, and are the perfect recipe for viral content. If you naturally have a talent for making your friends laugh or if you want to curate memes across the web, then this might be a great niche on Instagram.

Travel

Travel is huge on Instagram. Some of these accounts have massive followings, and all they do is post breath-taking pictures of a place you've never even heard of and probably can't afford to travel to. That's probably why people follow these accounts. It gives them a sense of adventure, something aspiration, and a form of escapism from their little cubicle. These types of accounts bring the best the world has to offer to the travel enthusiast. If you are the one who loves to travel or dreams of traveling full time, starting an account of your own is a great idea. Share your travel pictures, experiences, and love for our planet with the Instagram community, and they will reward you with lots of engagement.

Motivational quotes

Another super popular niche that anyone can start is motivational. If you're a fan of collecting inspiring and motivational quotes from the greats, then, by all means, go for it. Some of the accounts on Instagram have gathered together crazy followings by posting beautiful quotes that make people feel good. It's like a fast espresso shot for personal development addicts.

Crafts and DIY

Have you always had a knack for fixing things yourself? Do people call you when they need a homemade remedy of some kind? Then you might want to consider creating an account where you share your passion and skills. DIY accounts are pretty awesome and garner decent followings. Building things with your own hands and sharing it with your tribe isn't just rewarding. It's also a great way to monetize your account.

If you've gone through this list and felt utterly out of place because none of it resonates with what you want to create on Instagram, don't despair just yet. While I encourage you to pick a niche with an existing audience that is large enough, I'm aware that certain niches have small followings yet still work. So, if none of the above felt hot enough to you, check out a few examples on Instagram accounts that are doing really well even though they serve a tiny audience.

FAMOUS INSTAGRAM ACCOUNTS IN VARIOUS NICHES

If you usually geek out on topics and hobbies that leave your family members confused, these accounts should encourage you to go after your kind of people and make your Instagram account a success story.

Vegan and plant-based food

Food is a massive category on Instagram, but veganism isn't. Yet one can create a pretty healthy audience and get Instagram famous just from this niche. A great example is Kate Jenkins, who has an account dedicated to vegan recipes that are easy to make. She gets a decent engagement with every post.

Another great example is dietician Catherine (plantbasedrd), who shares easy vegan recipes as the handle suggests. With 300K followers and posts getting upwards of 4,000 likes each, Catherine is an excellent example of how a small niche can pay off big time.

https://elisedarma.com/blog/tiny-niches-instagram

Cute dog turned entrepreneur

I didn't make up that title. I snagged it from jiffpom, who has become an influencer on Instagram with over 10million followers. He has even won awards and gets featured on media outlets such as Fox News.

If you've got a cute pet that can entertain your audience, why not niche down to that?

Disney

I bet you didn't see that one coming! Yes, Disney themed Instagram account is a real niche. It's tiny, but that doesn't mean it won't make you money and get you real followers. For example, Kait Killebrew has an account focused purely on Disney. Instead of a regular travel account, she only talks about the Disney world. She's got over 5K followers, and sure, that doesn't make her a mega influencer, but it does give her enough influence to get paid sponsorship gigs.

Brands that sell products related to Disney now want to work with Kait because they know her audience is ideal, hyper-engaged, and loyal to that kind of lifestyle. It might seem crazy to think such a tiny niche is worth going after, but results don't lie.

Search Engine Optimization (SEO)

All businesses want to appear on the first page of Google. If your superpower and skill is showing others how to do this, why not create an account around SEO? You probably won't have crazy numbers as this is a smaller niche, but you can still do amazing in terms of engagement and income. For example, @conqueryourcontent focuses on all things SEO related. She has a following of over 2K, which makes her a micro-influencer. According to the SEO experts, the small following brings her high-quality leads, and she's consistently generating new projects each month from her Instagram marketing.

Whether you already have an account set up or not, now is the time to start building that right foundation. Let the examples and categories I've shared inspire you to choose the niche you will successfully work on over the coming months and years. To help you do it the right way, follow the steps below.

HOW TO CHOOSE YOUR NICHE THE RIGHT WAY

Step #1: Begin with your passions, talents, and skills.

As I said earlier, you're going to be doing this for a long time. Before that account can generate influence and revenue for you, there will be a lot of time, resources, and energy investment on your end, so it makes sense to do what you already enjoy.

That's why you need to identify your strengths, passions, and interests. Make this process impactful by going through the following questions with me. You can write the answers on a Google document or a notepad. List as many as you can think of.

- What topic do you most enjoy talking about with friends and family? I mean, you could go on for hours if they'd let you.
- How do you like to spend your free time?
- What hobbies have you had since childhood?
- What did you want to do when you were 9? Perhaps selling lemonade or creating comic characters?
- What topics do you enjoy learning? Look at the blogs, magazines, and social media accounts you follow.
- What skills have you trained on that you feel you're really good at?
- Is there something people love to get your advice on? It could be make-up tips, movie recommendations, or whatever else comes to mind.

Step #2: Do competitive research.

Once you identify what you're interested in posting, do a little research on Instagram to see what similar accounts are doing and their audience's response. Since you will share similar audiences, this is a great way to figure out what works and what doesn't. It also helps you identify potential brands you might work with once your brand is established if you're an influencer. At this point, your intention is to find popular accounts and the best hashtags on Instagram for your content. You can also use a site like all-hash-tags.com to find the best hashtags for your topic. For example, I typed in "Leadership" on the site and got 30 of the best hashtags.

Influencer tip:

If you already know a specific brand that you want to work with further down the road, make sure to research the influencers they are currently using. Follow these influencers and note the campaigns they create, the hashtags, and the type of content they put out. Learn as much as you can and do your best to create content geared toward that brand's interests and mission.

Step #3: Find the gaps

The next important step as you move toward defining your niche is to find gaps that you can fill in terms of content. Is there a topic that you feel isn't getting the attention it deserves? For example, if you want to do a vegan recipe account, maybe you can focus more on organic cruelty-free products because no one is doing that. That can be a great way to create a name for yourself within a broader category.

Step #4: Research what your ideal audience cares about

Remember that list of passions, talents, and skills? It's time to match it up with an audience. This will help you shortlist the best niche faster than any other step. It's also one of the most crucial steps you can take because it focuses on serving your future audience. Of course, if you have no audience or customer base, this exercise will require a lot more research and some gut guidance. What it comes down to is answering a few questions. Namely:

- What problem or challenge is my ideal client-facing?
- What desire or aspiration does my ideal client have?
- What values do we share in common?
- What type of content do they most care about?

If you start from zero and have no access to an existing audience, consider visiting forums and sites like Quora to see what people are discussing around your topic. You should also explore Google Trends, BuzzSumo, and Ubersuggest to uncover the search terms people are typing in related to their pain points as well as the social media content that's doing well on the Internet. If you don't know who your audience is or what's going on with them, the next chapter will guide you by finding your ideal audience and creating persona documents to help with your marketing campaigns.

The purpose of this particular exercise is to find an overlap between what you enjoy talking about and what your future followers care about. That point of intersection should be 70% of your content ideas and determine your page's theme.

Step #5: Make it beautiful

Instagram is all about attractive pictures, and your feed should have a look and feel that's appealing to your ideal audience. That doesn't mean going overboard and exaggerating or doing anything out of integrity with your personality (no need to get half-naked or show us your butt!). What it means is regardless of your niche, you need to choose a great color scheme, font, filters, and mood boards that will create an appeal for your audience. I don't care if your account is on health insurance or home repairs; think out of the box and visit beauty blogs, lifestyle blogs, and other Instagram accounts that have that wow factor. See what you can learn from them and apply what you learn to your topic.

Step #6: Figure out whether you can make money with your niche.

Unless you're doing this as a non-profit, this step should be done before proceeding to the next chapter. I want to assume that you've narrowed down your list to one or two topic areas as a result of the previous steps. It's a good idea to check out the income-earning potential of each of those niche topics so you can see which one will yield a higher return on investment for all your hard work. A great place to find answers is ClickBank, but you can also go to Amazon if that feels more comfortable. ClickBank is my top recommendation because you can find almost every niche and category one might think of. There are different offers for these categories, and the more products you find for a particular topic, the more confident you can be that it's a profitable niche. If you find nothing, then it probably means there's no monetizable crowd. You might be able to build an audience around that topic but earning money from it will be a huge challenge.

Step #7: Decide and stick with your niche

At this point, based on all your research and reflection, you need to decide if you'll move forward with your niche idea. Here's the deal; no one can make this decision for you. And once you make that decision, you have to stick with it long enough to see results. Now, that doesn't mean that every post should be on soufflés if that's your thing, but it does mean that a new follower should have the experience and immediately make the connection that you specialize with making great soufflés. So, your brand identity over time should become easier to connect with for both new and existing audiences as they interact with your content. Instagram influencers need to create consistency and stick to a niche if they want to make a good living out of it.

By following these steps, you now have a solid idea of what niche your account will focus on. This narrowed focus will enable you to build a name for yourself and experience growth quicker than trying to speak to everyone on Instagram. But there is one more important thing you need to invest time in before creating fantastic content that draws in followers. Head over to the next chapter to see what I mean.

4

DO YOU KNOW YOUR IDEAL AUDIENCE?

*Y*ou've probably heard that Instagram is one of the most popular social networks on the planet. It's actually ranked 6th in the world, with 1 billion users only surpassed by Facebook (2.6 billion), YouTube (2.0 billion), WhatsApp (1.6 billion), Messenger 1.3 billion), and WeChat (1.1 billion). The best part is that Instagram has a huge global audience. But having an international audience doesn't mean you can serve everyone on the platform. So before starting our content strategy for Instagram, we need to investigate more the behavior of the users to figure out what your ideal audience likes to experience on the platform so that your content can move in that direction. You have chosen your niche and already know what problems, aspirations, and topics your audience finds exciting, but how do you align that with content creation? By getting into the mind of your ideal fan. You must first begin by understanding who they are and their psychological state when browsing the platform.

INSTAGRAM USERS STATISTICS YOU SHOULD KNOW

We all behave and set different expectations for the various platforms we hang out in. When I am on YouTube, my mindset is different than when I am on Tik Tok or Instagram. The same is true for your ideal audience, so it's essential to understand the basics of how users behave on Instagram and what content is most appealing to them. Here are some useful stats that you should know from 2020.

- There are 500 million daily active users accessing the app globally.
- People spend an average of 28 minutes a day on the Instagram app. Users under 25 years spend even more time on the app, with data showing the younger demographic spending 32 minutes while those over 25 years spend 24 minutes.
- The most popular countries with the highest usage include United States (120 million), India (80 million), Brazil (77 million), Indonesia (63 million),

and Russia (44 million). There are 500 million daily active users accessing the app globally.

- 22.02% of the world's 4.54 billion active Internet users are accessing Instagram every month.

- In the United States, 75% of people aged 18 - 24 years use Instagram, followed by 57% who are between 25 - 30 years old.

- Globally, gender use is pretty even, with 50.9% being female and 49.1% being male users.

- In the United States, adult users are 43% women and 31% men.

- Brands typically look to brands with 50,000 to 100,000 followers to promote their products. This number, however, can be less depending on niche and industry.

- According to the 2020 data, the best time to post on Instagram is between 10:00 pm and 2:pm Central Daylight Time. The best days are Wednesday at 11:00 am, and Friday between 10:00 am to 11:00 am.

- Instagram images get an average of 23% more engagement than Facebook.

- Posts with videos receive 38% more engagement than photos.

- 70% of users look up brands on Instagram.

- 79% of users search Instagram for information on a product or service.
- 80% of users follow at least one brand on Instagram.
- One-third of Instagram users have purchased through the platform on mobile.
- 70% of consumers want to see brands they like and follow, taking a stand on social issues that matter to them. Out of those, 65% want the brands to take that stand on social media.
- The average engagement rate for branded posts is 4.3%.
- Having at least one hashtag can increase engagement by up to 12.6%.
- Longer hashtags get more results. The debate is still on, but so far, the magic number is 11 hashtags for each post if you want optimum results.
- 400 million users watch Instagram Stories daily.
- 46% of Instagram Stories users like funny and entertaining content.
- Brand Stories have an 85% completion rate.

SHOULD YOU PAY ATTENTION AND LEVERAGE YOUR INSTAGRAM COMPETITORS?

The simple answer is yes and no. Yes, if you have the right intention and strategy, these accounts can become a great source of information, inspiration, and lead generation. No, if you're coming from a place of lack mentality and only want to copy others.

Instagram has plenty of people to turn into followers, so you should never feel intimidated by the fact that you will find influencers and profile accounts already established in your chosen niche. I encourage you to see this as a good thing. Think about it. Finding an account with an already established audience of people who would also benefit from your content makes it a little easier for you to grow your account as long as you do it the ethical way.

You can growth hack your Instagram account by networking, following, engaging with, and establishing relationships with influencers in your space. Find authority content and choose the most important accounts that resonate with you and show signs of an engaged audience. I suggest making a list of 10 accounts and researching the following:

- What is their follower count?
- How often do they post?
- What engagement do they get on average?
- What theme can you identify from their feed?
- How often do they post Instagram Stories and IGTV?
- What hashtags are they using the most? What's the number count of hashtags used on each post?
- What is their branding like? For example, observe their tone of voice, colors, fonts, filters, messaging, and so on.
- What do they like posting about? Are there any gaps in the type of content they are posting that you can post on your feed?

The purpose of your competitor analysis is to learn as much as you can from your competition so that you can deploy the following tips.

1. Consider doing an outreach campaign to all the accounts that resonate with you and propose a collaboration.
2. Comment, like, share, save, repost, follow, and even create content mentioning the content you like from a competitor. Then tag them. And when you do comment on a photo or video, make it

thoughtful and valuable to the community so other users can experience your personality as well.

3. Consider offering to manage their account for free so you can promote your content. If you pick the right accounts with a decent following, high engagement, and no corresponding blog or website, the owner will likely accept your proposal. Although this strategy will involve more effort, it also opens you up to an already established audience, meaning you can exponentially grow your following within a matter of days or weeks.

4. If you're going to run some paid ads, I encourage you to find a competitor with a healthy audience size and run ads against him or her. If you use this approach, polish up your Instagram profile and bio to create some resonance so that they can immediately feel a connection with you. For example, if the competitor is local, consider adding your city name to your profile.

Bonus tip:

If you want to really dig your heels in with an organic strategy that doesn't cost a dime, here's a cool hack. Follow 100 of your top competitors' followers. After you follow someone, make sure to browse through their feed and find between one and three posts that you can heart and comment on. Make that comment thoughtful, and don't be afraid to use some emojis and your unique personality. It will take some upfront investment of time and energy, but I can assure you at least a 34% follow back result just by applying this simple hack.

TARGETING YOUR AUDIENCE

Everything hinges on our ability to determine with great accuracy who your content will be created for. If we miss the mark on producing content that engages a specific group of people from the one billion Instagram users, it will be next to impossible to monetize your account. The statistics I have shared with you in this chapter prove that an abundance of active users are already hanging out on the platform every day. Unfortunately, that doesn't mean they will be engaging with and buying from your brand. So how do we play to ensure the odds are in your favor? By investing a ton of time defining your target audience and continually carrying out tests to learn more about your tribe.

The first thing you should do is implement proven tactics that get this done. Suppose you don't have an existing customer base and no business data to go by or followers from other social media platforms to leverage; what then?

Start where you are, with what you know. Ask yourself the following questions:

- Who is my product or service designed for?
- What is my ideal audience looking for?
- What conversation is taking place on my competitor's account that can give me a glimpse of what my ideal audience wants more of?

Use a tool like Phlanx Influencer Auditor to provide you with insights such as demographics, brand mentions, follower locations, and engagement levels. That will enable you to see missing audience segments you've missed out on and the type of content your people might like as well as the most active follower locations for your type of product or service.

The next thing you want to do is monitor your Instagram analytics as you publish and interact with your community. Instagram can tell you a lot about your target audience, especially if you have a business account. If you don't know how to switch to a business account, I will demonstrate it in an upcoming section. Once you've been operating under the right type of account for a while, data will populate your Instagram insights, which can be accessed by going to the "Insights" tab > "Audience." You'll get to learn more about your existing followers and their location, gender, age-range, and so on. Add this information to the document you've been filling in so far, and you'll have a healthy understanding of what your target audience looks like.

Once you have an idea of your target audience, it's time to reach out. All the data you've gathered won't mean a thing if you don't put it to good use by creating content specific to that user group and engaging them within the community. For instance, you could start by identifying those hot hashtags that your ideal audience frequently use. These hashtags should be included in your post where appropriate. You should also invest some time daily clicking on those hashtags to find top-performing content so you can comment, like, and interact with others who have commented. Get your voice heard and share your opinion where you find trendy conversations in your niche. That can help you get noticed by all the right people. A neat trick is to sign up for a social listening tool that allows you to receive notifications of topics getting a lot of attention on social media.

Another thing you can do is connect with the right influencers in your space. Create irresistible incentives for the influencers that serve your ideal audience. You can find these influencers through hashtag research, as mentioned before, or by using platforms like Influencer.co. The only way this will yield positive results is if you plan ahead on the offer for the partnership. Do you have a great product or service you can give out for the influencer to review? Can you partner up for a giveaway contest or have them do a take-over of your Instagram for a set time period. You need to figure out what will be appealing to the influencer. When starting out, stick to micro-influencers as they are more likely to find your offer valuable. They are also easier to reach.

Suppose you have created a must-have skincare product that's organic, homemade, and really works to heal acne. But you have no Instagram following. Using the tips you've learned so far, you come across a beauty influencer who reviews organic make-up for sensitive skin. She's only got 20,000 followers and has really high engagement. This would be a perfect influencer for you to tap into because her audience would likely find your homemade organic skin acne healer very appealing. All you'd need is to make the influencer an offer she cannot refuse—something that benefits her, and her audience way more than it benefits you.

Now, get creative and think of how to apply this to your actual niche.

5

BRANDING YOUR INSTAGRAM ACCOUNT

*I*f you don't have an Instagram account set up, now is the time to do it. I will walk you through the simple process, and you can always reference the Instagram help center for any snags or new updates. Even if you have an Instagram account, I still suggest going through this entire chapter. You can always pick up tricks and ideas on how to improve.

CREATING AN ACCOUNT

The first thing you need to do is download the app from the App Store or Google Play Store, depending on your smartphone. Once installed, tap the Instagram icon to open and click the "Sign Up"/ "Create Account" button to create a new account. Use your email address or phone number and tap

"Next." If you prefer using Facebook, then you have the option to sign up with your Facebook account. You'll then be prompted to log into your Facebook account if you're currently logged out. If you choose to register with an email or phone number, you will be required to create a username and password, fill out your profile info and then tap Next.

The default setting for all Instagram users is a personal account. We want to use it to build our brand and market our business, so we have to switch it to a business account and connect that account to a Facebook business page. To link to your Facebook accounts and share posts directly from Instagram to Facebook, you need to go to your profile and tap the menu icon. Then click the little cogwheel for "Settings" > "Account" > Linked Accounts > Facebook. Enter your Facebook Login details and pick the page you want to be associated with this account.

If you're wondering how to switch from a personal account to a business account, it's super easy. Go to your profile and tap the menu in the upper right corner. Then go to "Settings" > "Account" > "Switch to Professional Account" > "Business". Here you would need to add details such as business category (this should be chosen based on your niche) and contact information. Once information is filled in, then tap "Done."

Personal Versus Business Account

Do you know the difference between a personal and business account, or why we insist on making the switch to a business account?

Let's start with the fact that only with a business account will you have the ability to receive analytics from Instagram telling you more about your audience. That will enable you to know which posts are performing best, which viewers came through your chosen hashtags and how many of the accounts being reached are currently following you. You can also get insights into your audience demographics. A business account will give you access to a lot more premium features, such as the ability to add the "swipe up" feature once you get to 10,000 or more followers, and you also get a "contact" button so that people can call or email you directly from Instagram. With the launch of Instagram shop and Reels, having a business account has never been more essential because only with a business account do you get the chance to show up on the Explore page through your reels. And of course, having an in-built Instagram shop makes it fast and easy to get a follower to purchase something from you.

TIPS FOR SETTING UP YOUR PROFILE

Anyone can set up an Instagram profile within a few minutes but setting one up that attracts new followers is something that requires a lot of careful consideration. That's why I am sharing best practices for setting up your Instagram profile the right way.

Tip #1: Make sure you've switched to a business profile

We've already discussed the benefits of setting up your account as a business profile. You want anyone in the world to view your awesome feed and your posts to have a wider reach so anyone who resonates with your profile can instantly follow you. That's why this is among the most important things you can do when setting up your profile.

Tip #2: Use an appropriate image that authentically expresses you and your brand

If your brand is centered around you, i.e., a personal brand, I encourage you to use a real picture of yourself. Look at accounts such as Marie Forleo, Gary Vaynerchuck, and Tai Lopez for great examples of ordinary folks who have built successful Instagram accounts. More people resonate with them because they come across as approachable and real. You want the same perception with your personal brand.

However, if you choose to go the corporate route, then learn from accounts such as Hubspot, Buffer, and CoSchedule. Use a simple logo and make sure it aligns with your main website and the brand identity. You might choose to modify your primary logo to fit better with the platform's dimensions but don't deviate too much from the original look.

Tip #3: Choose the right username and Instagram name

Picking a name that's memorable, searchable, and aligns with your brand identity is actually not as easy as one might think. Be mindful of the name you settle for, especially if you're going for a username that's different from your real name or company name.

You have up to thirty characters for your handle, and there should be no symbols or spaces. This is the name people will use when they mention you in a comment or if they want to tag you in something, so choose wisely. If you can't find something simple and creative, you can always use your name instead of combined with your specialty, e.g., Suzie, who specializes in vegan cuisine recipes, can call herself Suze_veganlife or Vegan_Suzie. To edit your @username go to profile page > "Edit Profile." Click on the text or space next to the person icon and enter the desired username. One thing to note is that you can change the Instagram name as often as you like to test out different titles that communicate what your audience will resonate it. However, I don't recommend regularly changing your username because you'd have to change all the places you added or linked to this username. Otherwise, people will get a "broken link" or error page when they click on your old links.

Tip #4: **Make your bio informative and engaging**

Your bio on Instagram is the description that shows up at the top of your profile. It's what new visitors will see when they first encounter your profile. Depending on that first impression that your words make, a user is more likely to browse through your feed, engage with your account, and ultimately follow you, or he or she will simply click away. The copy on this bio is, therefore, critical. You only have 150 characters to let people know what you're about and why they should follow you. That's not a lot of space to fully express yourself, so you need a lot of creativity to make this work. The best way to approach this is to think from the perspective of your potential follower. He or she lands on your profile either because they found your post through a hashtag they follow or some other reason. Now, what should your bio profile say to make this person more interested in adding you to his or her feed? What's in it for them? Why should they care about your account? How will you improve their world and make them feel better?

As you come up with your ideas, don't be afraid to add in your personality and play around with relevant emojis so people can "feel" the tone of your brand identity. An example I really like is from Oreo's Instagram account. On their profile, they write, " See the world through our OREO Wonderfilled lens." You can also check out Nike. They regularly tweak their bio, but I especially like " Spotlighting athlete and 👟 (Sport shoe icon) stories."

Tip #5: Make the most of your clickable link.

You've got one chance to direct people to your website or offer, so don't waste the link on your bio. That link is perhaps one of the most valuable real estate space you've got for driving traffic to your special product or service. If you want to keep things super simple, you can use a standard link from your landing page and regularly update it with the latest offers. Savvy Instagrammers are using tools like Tailwind to take things a step further and create a link that features multiple things. Regardless of which option you go for, track that link to gain data about the users clicking to learn more about your brand.

Tip #6: Create an attractive grid on your feed

Why is this important? Well, think about it. As soon as we discover a new account, we check out the profile pic, bio and then instantly scroll down to browse the feed. If our eyes and emotions resonate with what we see, it's an instant attraction, and we are likely to engage with and follow that account. If the feed repels us, it doesn't matter how much we liked the profile pic and bio; we'll likely click away without becoming a follower.

Often, I have come across a post while browsing a hashtag that matters to me and clicked through to check out more from the account. Once there, I become disinterested in the account because the rest of the feed doesn't speak to me. Most Instagrammers don't realize how many followers they might be losing purely because they don't invest some time thinking through their grid layout.

It's almost like cooking the best ingredients and serving them on an unappetizing plate. No one will want to eat that food. So, consider this exercise just as important as creating great content and writing good copy for your bio. To make sure you set yourself up for success, craft a pattern following the already existing rows of threes that Instagram offers. Your content can repeat in multiples of three, six, nine, twelve, or whatever you like, and it will always look like there's an overarching pattern that will create a sense of symmetry and consistency. For example, on one of my Instagram accounts, I've followed this pattern by switching between white and colored backgrounds. So, post #1 is a white background, post #2 is a colored background, post #3 is a white background, post #4 is a white background, post #5 is a colored background, and so on. You could also go a different route if you sell a specific product by making every third post an image of that product. For example, if you sell puppy accessories, every third post could be an accessory. That would eventually create that sense of consistency on your grid.

Advanced tip:

If you're comfortable with color coordination, you could use color scheme coordination by paring similar tones and colors on your grid. Just make sure the transition is seamless. It's perfect for feeds that focus more on selfies and human portraits as the main subject.

HOW TO BRAND ON INSTAGRAM

Branding is a vast topic, so we will focus on the main technical things you need to know and implement for our beginner's journey. After all, it's going to be hard standing out if you in the ocean of fellow Instagrammers if people cannot immediately identify what you stand for and what makes you unique. So, when you think about branding, approach it from the standpoint of evoking a specific emotion and perception. It's about creating an experience for your followers and potential followers. So what experience do you want to create, and how do you want people to remember you? Are you fun? Clean and minimalist? Youthful and rebellious? Serious and formal?

Branding is all about storytelling, trust-building, and perception. It can't be rushed, and it won't happen overnight. Every post moves you along this journey, so it's necessary to clarify your vision for your Instagram page and the mission or reason for creating this. Always anchor yourself in these key foundational elements as you determine what brand you're building. Another thing you want to think about is the tonality and personality that you want people to experience. It would be awkward to have a comical feed and use a serious or impersonal tone. That lack of congruency in your branding would unconsciously throw people off. The same is true for the colors and fonts.

The colors, font, and imagery you use should paint this picture to a user in a matter of seconds.

Most people begin this journey of branding by creating a mood board. You can do this on a software like InVision for free.

The next thing you need is to decide on brand colors. Instagram is a 100% visual-based app that emphasizes aesthetics, so have some fun here. Be true to yourself and find color combinations that enable you to express who you are while remaining relevant to your brand's message and offer. Different colors and shades have a different impact on the consumer. Some are perceived as calming or youthful, while others come across as bold, rebellious, or even gothic. This step might take you anything from a couple of hours to several days. But try not to overthink it. A helpful resource that can guide you to choose the right color for your Instagram brand is Colors. Cafe. They even have a very inspiring Instagram account where they post various color pallettes with each color code listed to speed up your decision-making process. You can also check out Pantone on Instagram, where they share lots of cool ideas on how to mix and match color.

Once you've decided on a color, it's time to find the right font. Although the captions use a standard font on Instagram, your posts will require some text from time to time unless you only specialize in selfies. If you're doing a motivational account with quotes, this part of your branding is critical. The font you use instantly tells a story and reveals your personality. One thing I want to point out before encouraging you to pick a font is to be mindful of the type of font because while some of them are extremely cute, they can be tough to see or read on the Instagram feed. This is a mobile-first app, so everything needs to be ideal for the small screen.

The best and easiest to read on mobile are Serif, Sans serif, Display, and Modern. Serif fonts supposedly represent tradition, respectability, and discernment. San serifs are modern, objective, modern, and associated with innovation. Modern fonts are considered stylish and strong. Display fonts are often associated with friendliness, amusement, and expressiveness. To help you figure out what fonts you should use, consider using a design app like Canva, which has an enormous font library to play with. They even have ready-made templates and font pairings. You can also follow the Instagram account of welovebranding for some inspiration.

At this point, you already have your target audience honed in, as we discussed in the last chapter. Since you know who you will be creating content for, it's important to do a quick assessment to see if the branding specs you're going for aligning with your target audience. In other words, are the colors, fonts, mood boars, and so on something they would find attractive?

Examples of accounts that are crushing it with their branding:

Example #1: BulletProof

They are a coffee and nutrition supplement company. They have three things going for them regarding branding - minimalistic yet striking color scheme + simple images + uniform quote tiles to break up their feed.

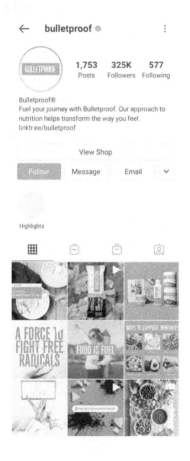

Example #2: Starface

It is an up-and-coming skincare brand that makes unique acne stickers in the shape of stars. That fits in perfectly with their bright yellow aesthetics, which is impossible to miss on your feed. Their theme is pretty consistent while posting testimonials, memes, and more. Bright and colorful is what they're sticking to, and it seems to be working given their 119K followers and counting.

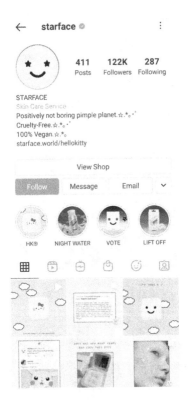

Example #3: Studiodiy

With over 400,000 followers, this account knows how to build an Instagram brand. It's colorful, whimsical, and feels like you're having a party. The feed is bold and fun, but don't be fooled; these guys have intentionally created this mood of "life is a party" by carefully curating their feed for maximum impact. The account uses a wide array of colors, but they disperse them thoughtfully to ensure no two side-by-side images look exactly the same. If you observe the feed carefully, you'll notice a running rainbow theme, which makes the aesthetics of the feed a great delight for the eyes as you scroll the posts. If you want to have this same bursting of color effect, just go for one or two bold primary colors and balance this out with a few pastel shades.

Before we move, here's a simple step-by-step to follow as you build your brand based on everything we've covered thus far.

Step #1: Begin with the end in mind. Set your objectives for Instagram.

Step #2: Narrow down your focus and choose a style pattern or theme for your feed.

Step #3: Identify your ideal audience and figure out what they care about.

Step #4: Create a killer profile and bio that speaks to them.

Step #5: Decide on the color scheme, font, and mood board for your feed.

Step #6: Identify your brand's tone and personality.

Step #7: Create awesome content.

SECTION 03: CREATING INSTAGRAM CONTENT

6

THE CONTENT PLAN

*a*s you saw in the previous chapter, creating awesome content is fundamental to building a successful brand on Instagram. This is where we will cover everything you need to know to create engaging posts and videos. The bottom line is that you need to start with the ideas you've gathered after going through previous audience research exercises, competitor research, and determining what you're passionate about. The content should be aligned with your vision, mission, and the theme of your feed.

When we discussed theme or style pattern, we emphasized things such as colors you'd use and the filters you'd like to apply to your images. It's time to add another component, and this is the type of content you will be posting.

Your niche is going to direct you on the type of posts to go for. Then, feel free to get creative when it comes to creating that harmonious and consistent feel. The visual appeal and style that you use should reflect your brand's identity. Once you nail that down, it's time to create a content plan.

The goals you set at the beginning of this book should inform the content you will create and publish. You also need to consider how much time will be assigned to content creation and publication. Unless you are fortunate enough to have a big team, you'll be doing all of this on your own until such a time that you're able to outsource. Please consider your current lifestyle, obligations, and whether this will be a full-time thing or a side hustle that you'll work on during weekends and late at night.

Take a moment to get honest about how much time you can commit to content creation each week. Then, mark it in your calendar so that you can block out that time and get it done. We'll discuss the different types of posts you can create and the best performing content on Instagram for a little inspiration.

STICKING TO YOUR NICHE

Here's a mistake many newbies make. Once they publish a few posts, they start getting distracted by what they see on other accounts and start to copy that, expecting it will get them results faster. Have you ever been to an account that felt overwhelming when you scrolled through the feed? That happens as a result of trying to appeal to everyone. The worst part about mixing up your themes on the feed is that you'll confuse your potential followers because they won't clearly identify what you stand for. And if your tribe cannot quickly identify you, they won't be sticking around long enough to become fans or customers.

Just because you see a cute puppy post getting lots of likes and attention on your feed doesn't mean you should switch to posting puppy pics when it has nothing to do with your brand.

The lesson here is on brand consistency. You already did the hard work of finding your niche, researching, and creating a content theme and plan for the type of content you'll be publishing. Do not deviate from your plan just because you don't see the results you expected. There is no such thing as an overnight success, so be patient with your plan and stick to your niche.

CHECK WHAT OTHERS ARE DOING.

From time to time, I think it's beneficial to check on your peers or influencers in your niche to see how they are growing their accounts. This can be used as a tactic for getting inspiration for your content and a hack for engaging with their followers who might also be interested in what you offer. Invest some time each month to go through the top ten people in your space and use social listening tools to inform you of their best performing content. Then, analyze it to figure out what's working and what the audience wants to see more of and challenge yourself to create something ten times better than what they have.

GETTING INSPIRATION

Piggybacking on the idea of getting content inspiration from those in your niche, you should also invest time for gathering inspiration for your content so that it remains fresh, relevant, and appealing to the Instagram audience. Here are a few places I find inspiration when planning out my content.

Google Alerts

This is an easy way to receive alerts from Google based on the terms you choose to monitor. By creating an alert on a specific topic, you'll receive email notifications on all the interesting and top-performing content across the web.

BuzzSumo

BuzzSumo software is one of the preferred tools for learning what's popular across social channels. It's a personal favorite, and the main reason is that I can easily find the most shared content across all social networks on my chosen topic here. I can even plug in a competitor's website and figure out their top-performing content. Once I find the top performers, I click to dig through the comments because I can often find lots of inspiration on what to create next.

Pinterest Boards

Given how visual Pinterest is, it can be a great source of inspiration for your Instagram content. Pinterest is great for curating content. Find a group board on your niche topic where you can find links and infographics. You can custom make your board and collect interesting articles. These articles are great for discovering what people want to see or learn more about.

Imgur

Not many know this platform, but it's a great place for getting visual content inspiration. Imgur showcases the most popular images on the web. This is perfect for an Instagrammer, especially if you're looking for memes, quotes, or humor.

The most important thing to remember is to remain on brand and stick to your theme as you gather these ideas. Just because something makes you laugh or swoon doesn't mean it should be added to your content plan.

Remember, inspiration comes from anyone and anywhere at any time. Always be on the lookout for ideas, stories, and insights that you feel will benefit your growing audience.

INSTAGRAM POSTS

Now that you have inspiration on what to post and a plan that aligns with your theme and vision, let's talk about the different types of posts known to perform well. Currently, Instagram allows images, videos, and carousels on the feed. But that doesn't limit what you can create within the context of an image, video, or carousel. Here are some popular content types.

#1: Motivation

This type of content can include videos of you inspiring and encouraging your audience or motivational quotes. Instagram users love getting encouragement from people with shared values and a powerful message. Some accounts have hundreds of thousands of followers, so if you're into speaking or have a powerful message to share, consider creating this form of positive content.

#2: Behind the scenes

This type of content gives your followers that exclusive inside look that makes them feel like they really know you. In many ways, this is your chance to show a more human and personal aspect of your brand. It's a great way to create real authenticity and connection, whether you're a personal brand or a large business.

#3: "How to" photos & videos

This type of content should be actionable and educational. How-to content is extremely valuable, and it performs well on Instagram. Whether you want to show your audience how to bake cookies, make a cocktail, or put on makeup the right way for different occasions, this content will attract the right tribe to you. You could also create a series of images showing your audience how to use a new feature of your software app.

#4: Giveaway

This type of content is usually part of a larger campaign. It is great for generating buzz and attracting potential followers and fans on Instagram. Why? Because people love free stuff! A giveaway post or video practically invites people to participate in something you've created so they can win something. It works because it encourages social sharing, and it's a fast way to grow your following. Just make sure you have a good plan behind it and that you give away something valuable to the audience while remaining relevant to your brand. For example, a golf brand should not give away an iPhone! Instead, something related to golf should be the main prize. See what I mean?

#5: Influencer takeover

You can partner up with an influence in your niche and have them take over and post content and Instagram Stories for a set time. It will attract a new audience, as it gives your account exposure to their audience. It also creates an excellent variety on your feed. This content is great for growing your follower and fan base if you have access to influencers.

#6: Posts featuring influencers

This type of post can either be created by you or by the influencer you are featuring. It works exceptionally well for eCommerce brands because if you can get someone influential to strut your product, you can show your followers how great your product is. Even if you're the one posting the image or video mentioning the influencer using your products, users love seeing well-known names endorsing your brand.

#7: **User-generated images and videos**

This type of post is among the best performing content when it comes to conversion. Although you don't create the content, you can incentivize people to make this type of content and share it with you so you can repost it on your feed. People are always more concerned about how your product or service can improve their lives, so this type of content produces excellent engagement. If you already have an existing customer base, this is content you can get immediately to boost your marketing campaign. Give the previous or existing customers an irresistible offer so they can create posts and tag you or use a particular hashtag so you can have this content easily accessible in one place, ready for curation and reposting.

FOCUS ON YOUR THEME AND VISUAL STYLE

In alignment with your content plan and sticking to your niche, it's also important to consistently maintain a theme that easily reminds people of what you stand for. We already talked about the importance of creating a coherent look and feel. This could be as simple as the color your use, how you crop the borders, the layout of the patterns, or a combination of some of these. Having that consistency trains new and potential followers into your unique style and helps them know what to expect from you. It makes it easier for them to spot your content on their feed, increasing the chances of engagement. Let's share some examples of what a great visual style should look like and some examples of popular Instagram themes, so you don't get stuck.

Clean Background

This type of theme is great for foodies or anyone who wants to emphasize details without distraction. By using this theme, your audience will be drawn more to the main subject of the photo. Lots of food bloggers use this theme on their feed. To make it work for you, it's recommended to get a space with an all-white backdrop and good lighting. This will cut down your editing time tremendously, and of course, you can use an editing app for the final touches.

Bright Whites

This is a hugely popular theme, especially for photographers and designers. It's fresh and clean and bright, which makes the feed harmonious and details really pop out. To create this kind of theme, you need to take most of your pictures in a bright white space with natural light. You can also use an editing app to help you get that bright, clean look. Then arrange photos with pops of color in a balanced way to even out the color balance in your feed.

Alternating Borders

This type of theme is quite popular on Instagram and easy to create. All you need to do is edit your photo in an app first. You can use Apps like InShot and A Color Story to frame your pictures.

Color Contrasts

If you love bold splashes or contrasting color, why not turn that into a theme? Yes, I know the norm is usually a single color, tone, or hue on a photo, but sometimes being bold can pay off. Check out @colormecourtney to see what I mean. Her feed is bold and full of vibrant energy. If you'd like something similar, then all you need to do is invest in an editing app that can help you turn on the volume of all the radiant hues you'll have. And of course, make sure to take pictures where you can find a lot of contrasting colors. As you publish your post, be mindful of the arrangement so you can balance out the visuals. A good rule of thumb is to switch up the placement of colors and to avoid blobs of one color dominating the feed. Go for that magical rainbow effect, and you will wow your audience.

INSTAGRAM CAPTIONS

Tell me if you've had this experience recently. You notice a post from your favorite celebrity, and you click on it to check out the full post. Then you realize the post (usually a selfie) has gathered thousands of likes and lots of attention. Yet, the celebrity didn't even post a single caption. It was just a cute or sexy looking selfie of themselves and their dog.

You might be inclined to assume your posts will attract just as much attention even if you don't say a word on your captions. You'd be dead wrong! Sure, if it's a half-naked picture of you with lots of right hashtags, you might get lucky and receive some attention, i.e., reach, but if you want engagement and conversion, you'll have to do better than just a half-naked selfie and twenty hashtags.

What you need are powerful captions. These are written copy carefully crafted to help you take your audience from curious and interested to seriously engaged in what you want them to know about your brand.

By the way, that celebrity who can get away with using zero captions on his or her post probably has millions of followers. So, getting a couple of thousand likes is feasible. Until you get to the point where people are so obsessed with your brand, they want to know what shake you had for breakfast, stick to creating posts with meaningful captions.

How do you create awesome Instagram captions?

Since Instagram is a highly visual platform, you don't have to become a copywriting expert. You don't even need lots of words. People are on this platform to feast with their eyes, and reading isn't such a high priority, so short and sweet will serve you better than long-winded rants.

The purpose of an Instagram caption is to tell more of the story behind your image or video post. Whether you do that in one catchy sentence or a few paragraphs, what matters is the message comes across clearly. Suppose the image or video is about a sale or event. In that case, your captions should give clear explanations and instructions on how to participate and where. If your post is about your business, make sure to share why this impacts your audience, who was involved in that particular post, maybe even celebrating team members if applicable.

BEST PRACTICES FOR WRITING INSTAGRAM CAPTIONS:

Focus on adding value, not the length of the caption.

There is no right or wrong length for your Instagram captions. Some accounts have long copy and still get high engagement. At the same time, others use a single sentence yet also have higher engagement rates. What matters is the value in the words written. Use that real estate to offer tips and share tricks or industry hacks. If you're talking about your business, make sure it is customer-centric and not self-promotional as much as possible. If you're sharing a back-story, add details that are relevant and appealing to your audience. The more you think about user experience, the easier it will be to create something that people want to heart, save, and even share with their friends.

Write like a human for a fellow human.

A mistake I see with some accounts is that they try to be formal and unnatural with is easy to spot. It comes across as fake, especially when the tone of the copy doesn't align with the theme and images on the feed. On Instagram, you want to come across as friendly and approachable as possible. Think of it like texting your friend. How would you communicate a message to him or her? That same authentic and natural flair is what you need to add to your Instagram captions. If you don't usually use big formal words when you speak to friends, don't do that on your Instagram feed.

Use a hook.

The first sentence of your captions should have an impact on the readers. This is what they will see before clicking on the more icon. Make it appealing, and you'll see better engagement.

Storytelling is the secret sauce for success.

Personality and storytelling on your captions will cause people to engage with you more. Don't be afraid to express your truth and spice things up with your own Vocabulary. If you check out accounts such as @HDFMAGAZINE, you will get a taste of what authentic expression looks like on Instagram. This brand is consistent with its theme, type of posts, and captions on each theme. They post long captions and still get fantastic engagement and interactions from their followers because they know how to use descriptive, emotional phrases and anecdotes in their captions.

Give each post caption a purpose and intention.

There should be a specific reason for writing your captions. That reason should align with your overall business objectives and the image or video's objective, which we addressed earlier. Therefore, you will know the purpose of the captions and encourage your followers to take appropriate action. You can add a call to action or ask a question so that your audience can enter a contest, shop for a specific product, ask you questions for engagement and live interactions, visit your website or follow your account. There's no end to the actions you can request from your audience as long as it's congruent with the image or video.

Examples of actions to add to your captions. "Click the link in bio," "Leave me a comment below with your answer," "Tag a friend who needs to hear/read/see/win this today."

Use emojis generously

Emojis on your Instagram captions add that extra flavor that animates your captions. It makes you look lighthearted and full of personality. You can also use emojis at the end of a sentence as a bookend or to break up a long-winded copy. Given the fun nature of the platform, you could even substitute certain words with relevant emojis. For example, instead of writing the word "books," you can use 📚. The only thing to be mindful of is the amount of emojis you use. Don't overdo it, and make sure whichever you use aligns with your tone of voice.

If you're looking for some inspiration on emojis that call attention to a call-to-action, here's what I like to use: 👋 👆 📌 🎯 🔗

Examples of Instagram captions to give you inspiration:

Funny Instagram Captions.

Namast'ay in bed.

We don't know what's tighter: Our jeans or our company culture.

Friday... My second favorite F word.

I'm just a girl standing in front of a salad, asking it to be a cupcake.

Business Instagram Captions.

At [your company name], our best asset is our people.

Big things often have small beginnings. [Your Business Name] 's story began right here in this basement.

Sassy Instagram Captions

I got 99 problems, but an awesome marketing team ain't one.

It's not called being bossy. It's called having leadership skills.

I'm an acquired taste. If you don't like me, acquire some taste.

Take a moment now to think about the type of captions you'll be creating for your first posts. Are you going to come across as funny? Inspirational? Serious? Sassy? Controversial?

HASHTAGS GALORE

Although Twitter was the first platform to officially adopt hashtags back in 2009, the first hashtag's origin back in 2007 is credited to Nate Ridder. He used #sandiegoonfire in his social messages to inform people about the wildfires his local area was experiencing at the time. Fast forward to 2021, and hashtags dominate many of the social platforms, especially Instagram. I'm sure you know and use particular hashtags, and you've heard marketers encouraging Instagrammers to use hashtags as a way to increase reach. But do you know the real purpose of using a hashtag?

Hashtags are meant to help us group similar content together. That makes it easier for the right person to find the right content at the right time with the least amount of effort. Another of looking at it is through the lens of like attracts like. People with similar interests will flock together around a topic they resonate with. Your brand should create content that enables your tribe (people interested in your topic) to learn more about your product, campaign, and the informative content you have.

On Instagram we help the algorithm sort through our content and deliver it to the right people through the hashtag system. Currently, the most popular hashtags on Instagram are #picoftheday, #photooftheday, #love, #fashion, #beautiful, #instagood, #happy, #cute, #tbt, #like4like, #followme, #selfie, #me, #summer, #friends, #repost, #nature, #girl, #fun, #style, #food, #instalike, #family, #travel, #life, #beauty, #nofilter, #amazing, #instamood, #instagram, #photography, #fitness, #smile, #instadaily, #art

How To Create Your Branded Hashtag

This option is only favorable once you've grown a decent size following. The more people engage with you and become familiar with your brand, the more likely they will start using your brand's hashtag. It's also great to create give-aways and contests because people can add a specific campaign hashtag to participate. The bigger your brand becomes on social media, the more people will start using your hashtag, making it easier to do social listening.

When you decide on a hashtag for your brand, make sure it's brief and unique to your brand. It should evoke a specific emotional reaction that you've deliberately chosen. Whether offline or online, if you run events, it's a good idea to create a hashtag specific to that event. Don't be afraid to incorporate a bit of humor and clever-ness if it aligns with your brand and topic. I've seen some big flops whereby brands went too far and either didn't research the hashtag well enough or forgot to consider whether there was a hidden meaning behind their chosen hashtag that would come across as unappealing. The most important thing is to know your audience and how they perceive your business so you can use the right tone when you come up with something catchy. Regardless of how sassy your brand is, be thoughtful about the hashtags you create and think long term association and perceived reputation. I love seeing branded hashtags like #ShareACoke or #justdoit, so once you have an active audience, consider coming up with your own branded hashtag.

BEST PRACTICES FOR CHOOSING HASHTAGS

I recommend creating a healthy mix of popular and super niched hashtags to boost your account growth. For example, #love is huge, with 1.9 billion posts. Getting your content noticed with that hashtag is going to be a huge challenge. So, the best thing you can do is combine that hashtag with others that have less volume and competition. A great way to determine what to pair it with is to use a hashtag generator tool such as All Hashtag or Hashtagify. You can also do keyword research using Google or Ubersuggest. Longtail hashtags might perform better as long as you know this is a phrase the user is typing. In addition to using the popular keyword mentions, you could also add #loveisintheair, #lovestory, #lovepuppies, #lovelife, #lovinglife, #lovethis,

#lovenature, or another combination which better suits your content.

Aside from using a handful of popular hashtags, you can also use trending hashtags but again, make sure it's relevant. For example, if it's a summer sale, then, of course, #summer and #sale will work best. If you have something unique to offer for a special occasion or create content specific to a holiday, be sure to use the appropriate hashtag. For example, use #valentinesday in February and #Christmas in December as these hashtags trend during those specific months.

Pro tip:

If you want to get the most out of this hashtag strategy, you can follow a hashtag and location tag that's linked to your niche and interact with the participants. For example, if you're an up-and-coming Instagram influencer, you can find events for social media marketing or small business networking events for digital marketing.

PLANNING YOUR POSTS

Instagram is a highly visual platform with plenty of competition, so if you fail to plan out your content properly, then you're essentially setting yourself up to fail. So, the next important step to take now is to map out on a calendar or template the kind of content you will create over the next 90 days. If you're more artistic or simply enjoy mood boards, now is the time to create one. If you enjoy excel or Google spreadsheet, then use that to curate and map out the categories, topic, and type of post you will create.

Here's what you need on your spreadsheet: Date of publication, Time, Content file name or link (if it's an uploaded video), The link that'll be added to the bio section, Image caption, Hashtags, Goal/Campaign.

Create a new page on your spreadsheet for Instagram Stories as well so you can monitor this separately.

Decide how much content will be created and how much will be curated, then gather the necessary content and start filling in your planner. Since this is a new account and you're still learning the ropes, allow yourself to be flexible with the content type of content. You might start off assuming your audience will be attracted to your account mainly for bite-sized educational content but then quickly realize the best performing posts are beautiful aesthetically focused content or maybe user-focused content. Watch your content performance from month to month to determine how to adjust and what content to create more of. Some key things to look for include the number of new followers you're gaining from one month to the next, number of people liking, commenting, and saving your content.

Another thing you want to include as you plan the content is some variety. Images alone won't cut it in 2021. You need to experiment with videos and other cool graphics as well. Don't forget to maintain a consistent visual theme even when testing video. Pay attention to the colors, filters, fonts, and style patterns, as we mentioned earlier.

TOOLS FOR PLANNING AND SCHEDULING YOUR POSTS

To make this process easier manageable, you can use planning tools and scheduling tools. You can create a spreadsheet for visual planning, as I just mentioned, for free, or get a tool such as Later, Asana, Trello, or any other productivity tool with the content calendar feature. The most recommended scheduling tools include Buffer, HubSpot, Later, Meet Edgar, and Sked. Although most of the tools only allow you to post a single image, you can go for a software like Sked with lets you post Stories and Carousels if you have a bit of a budget.

Instagram Guides

Instagram launched a new format for sharing curated, scrollable content called Instagram Guides and they are quickly gaining popularity. It's a new way of putting out helpful recommendations and tips and although it started as a way for Instagram to allow people in healthcare and other wellness advocates to provide resources during the COVID-19 pandemic, it's now available to all users.

You can access this feature by taping the plus icon on the top right of your profile page and selecting "Guide" at the bottom of the list. Once you click on it, three formats will pop up i.e., places, products and posts.

Places recommends places in your city and beyond.

Products recommends your favorite products. Super handy for Instagram influencers and affiliate marketers.

Posts recommends the posts you have created or saved.

As you can see, there's a tremendous opportunity for you as a creator to add value and build authority with your audience. For example, a post guide can be used to create a thread of Instagram posts that you previously created or saved with a custom headline and extra commentary. Use this to enhance your story-telling strategy. You can also offer useful advice or guidance. If you open up an Instagram Shop you can also use the Products option to curate some of your best offers.

HOW TO USE INSTAGRAM GUIDES TO GROW YOUR BRAND AND BUSINESS

This is an incredibly powerful tool for doing value-first marketing. Whether you are an Instagram Influencer or a small business owner, think creatively about serving your potential customer and new followers. What kind of content, advice or guidance would benefit them that can also lead to business for you?

For example, if you're the owner or manager of a restaurant or café, creating Guides for "Places" is a great for sharing location-based recommendations such as city guides, where to eat etc. You can also curate your posts with the latest menu or Chefs recommendation. In other words, you are only limited by your creativity and willingness to put in the effort to create the guides.

For eCommerce stores, having a Product guide can enable you to showcase your bestsellers and get people to buy more than ever.

To access an Instagram Guide, go to your profile or a user's profile page and select the new Guides icon from the feed tab. By clicking on that icon, you will see all the guides created by the owner of that account. You can also easily share them to your Instagram Stories by tapping on the paper plane icon at the top right-hand corner of the screen.

7

TAKING GREAT PICTURES FOR YOUR INSTAGRAM ACCOUNT

*L*et's focus on the technical aspects of creating a successful brand on Instagram. As stated several times, this is a visual-first platform. So, it makes sense to give you some hacks on how to make your photos pop on the feed. If you're in an industry that photographs well, such as beauty, food, and travel, then, of course, you'll have an easier time creating awesome content as long as you get the right equipment. We'll talk about what equipment you can use on a budget shortly. But what if you're in a niche that doesn't photograph well? What if your topic is dull and lacks that aesthetics appeal?

All is not lost. I've come across really creative accounts from niches most of us consider absolutely dull such as personal injury, life insurance, investment banking, and I could go on and on. One thing I've noticed about "boring brands" that succeed well on Instagram is the approach they use. Most of these accounts don't try to be something they are not. Instead, they go with the flow and create a feed that is aesthetically pleasing to amass a large following. The images they use are somewhat relevant to the main idea of what they do; however, they don't focus at all on selling their product or service. Instead, they just want to grow a strong online presence with a large following.

For example, I came across a beautiful motivational feed that shared stunning nature pics and motivational quotes on life lessons. I loved the account so much that I followed that account. Soon after, I got a welcome message followed by a video from the account owner, who it turns out is a lawyer. He curates quotes and takes beautiful nature pics to draw attention and then builds a relationship from there. Of course, his conversion may not be as high as a food blogger. Still, given that he has 300K followers, I'm pretty sure he's able to convert enough clients for his personal injury services. That's a classic example of how far a little creativity can serve you on Instagram. So regardless of your niche, you can succeed on Instagram. It begins with taking great pictures.

WHAT SPECIAL EQUIPMENT TAKES GREAT PICTURES FOR INSTAGRAM?

The truth is you don't need a special camera to take an Instagram worthy picture that will grow your channel. Some Instagrammers have become influencers and amassed huge followings with images from an iPhone. In contrast, others have invested thousands of dollars in equipment and a stunning studio setup. There is no right or wrong. Start where you are with the tools at hand.

The most important thing about your picture is the editing and the intention behind the picture. However, I will share a small list of things you can invest in if your budget allows it.

#1. A camera you know well enough.

While it's great to upgrade your tech and invest in expensive cameras, it's better to start with what you know. You can use a smartphone, a mirrorless camera, or a DLSR.

Mirrorless cameras are smaller, lightweight, and have more modern features. DSLR are heavier, larger in size with a longer and better battery life and better autofocus systems.

A smartphone can also do the trick, especially if you're working with the latest iPhones or Android mobiles. Smartphones like iPhone 11 Pro, Google Pixel 4, and Samsung S20 are great choices if you want to stick to mobile photography.

It also makes the editing and posting process super simple, especially once you learn of the latest software that can turn your images from good to extraordinary. You can also get an iPhone Lenses if you want to enhance the image. Consider getting the Moment lenses, which give you a wide-angle or telephoto effect. This is great for Instagram Stories as well. The most important thing is learning to use all the features on your smartphone. There's a lot of information on YouTube that can show you how to take the best pictures from your smartphone. TechSpot has a great article, which I will link to in the resource page that shares tips for taking great pictures using a smartphone.

If you want a great mirrorless camera, then consider getting the Sony a6100. It has a fantastic screen for shooting with live view and does 11 frames per second RAW shooting and 4K video. It also has eye detection autofocus. The best part for a beginner is with the a6100, you'll be able to take photos high up or low to the ground without laying on the ground thanks to its tilting LCD screen on the back. The screen flips over the top, making selfies and vlogging super easy. One more thing to mention is the camera is Wi-Fi included, which is something every beginner needs to make image exporting faster. If you have an Android phone, this camera has NFC built-in to transfer photos with a tap, so if you have the budget and can afford to invest about $848, this is a great entry point.

Do you prefer Canon instead? How about experimenting with Canon Rebel T3i, which also has excellent features, including a screen that swivels around, making selfies super easy.

For a DSLR camera, my recommendation is Canon T6i, which comes with a flip screen and a touch screen. It comes with a 242 Megapixel CMOS (APS-C) sensor, ISO 100-12800 (expandable to H:25600), and the EOS Full HD Movie mode helps capture brilliant results in MP4 format. You can also check out Canon 80D and M50, which also come with dual pixel autofocus. Why is that important? If you're going to be shooting in live view a lot, a DSLR camera with dual pixel autofocus will serve you best. The T6i doesn't come with dual pixel autofocus. Still, it does have built-in Wi-Fi so you can easily edit and upload to Instagram.

#2. Great lighting equipment

The best lighting is always going to be natural sunlight. So, if you have no budget to invest in lighting equipment but live in a sunny location, then you have everything you need for that perfect Instagram shot. However, if your budget allows you to invest in some lighting equipment, consider getting some ring lights, which usually vary in prices. You can get some for as low as $20 or go for a softbox if you have the money. I started off with a Neewer 700W Professional Photography 24" X24"/60X60cm softbox with E27 Socket

Light Lighting Kit. And it goes for around $90, but it's well worth the price.

#3. Tripod

You will need a tripod to hold your camera (especially when doing selfies or Instagram Live). No one likes shaky images or videos, so this is a great way to ensure your pictures look professional. Depending on your camera, you can get a tripod that specifically holds your device in place. You don't have to spend a ton of money on this. A basic 60-inch tripod will do the work just fine.

#4. Remote

An inexpensive remote that pairs with your chosen camera wirelessly and can be used within 10 feet is a great investment if you're doing this solo. It will save you lots of running back and forth or using timers.

#5. A blank canvas and reflective surface

This is definitely optional but nice to have. Depending on whether you're a business doing mainly product images or a personal brand taking selfies and face-to-camera video recordings, you may want to invest in a blank canvas and a reflective surface for better quality production. For a reflective surface, I highly recommend using a foam board, which is cheap and works just as great as fancy professional studio equipment. To get the most out of your reflector, first, light your set up with the main light source, and then use the reflector to bounce any light back into the shadowy areas.

You can also get creative with blank canvas options and improvise with a foam board again or even a plain white wall if you're going for that traditional look.

Other extras to know about include a memory card, which is very handy if you choose to get a camera. I also suggest you get a camera strap and sleeve. These will protect you and the camera, especially If you're an active photographer. If you invest in a camera, one final tip is to get a great lens and perhaps even a secondary battery to make sure you're always prepared. Educate yourself on the various lens options available at a price point you can easily afford, and that also pair well with your camera choice. And that's it! Nothing too complicated, and you could even simply get started with a smartphone until your account gains enough momentum.

CAPTURING MOMENTS

If you're an active photographer and you want to make your feed all about action moments of people on the move, getting that right can be quite daunting. So how do you do it either for yourself or a friend?

Well, there are several options to consider. If you invested in a remote control for your camera, you could always set down the camera in the right spot and take the picture. Or, if you're doing a mid-action shot, you could either set a timer or record it as a video and then pause and screenshot that particular moment you want to capture.

The main thing to note is that action pics don't need to seem perfect and out of this world. What matters is the intention and story behind the picture. So, if you're celebrating completing a marathon or taking pictures of clients having fun with your products, or wearing your swag outdoors, focus less on making it perfect and more about capturing the right light. Lighting is what it comes down to when it comes to capturing moments. Consider doing action pictures during sunrise or sunset as that is the best time. This is, of course, mainly for photographers who are focused on outdoor images and content. But what if you want to focus on still photos at home? What's a good setup that's easy to create?

A SETUP FOR TAKING STILL PHOTOS:

Whether you're going to use your phone or a camera to take still photos, here are some tips to help you take still pictures like a pro.

Go for bright.

The best still pics are taken indoors with great natural light or outside in daylight. You just can't beat the clarity and crispness of colors that comes with using great natural light. Good light is the foundation of a great photo so take the time to study the device you'll be using.

Pro tip:

Light from the front is always going to be the most flattering. Light from the side makes your subject look more three-dimensional, highlights texture, and creates a moody effect; subjects lit from the back look dreamy and glowy.

Pick the right time for your photoshoot.

Nature has its own Instagram filter known as the golden hour by photographers. When the sun is low on the horizon, every photo looks more stunning. If you can plan your shoot at this time, then, by all means, take advantage. But even if you can't, then understand your limitations and what can work in your favor. For example, a midday shoot with plenty of clouds can work just as well if you know what you're doing.

Follow the rule of thirds

When taking a still picture, the rule of thirds is one of the most well-known composition principles. It divides an image into a 3x3 grid and aligns the subject or object in the photo along the grid lines to create balance. Some smartphones have an in-built grid to visually help you check your settings to see what's available. Turn on the gridlines for your phone camera to practice this before shooting.

Choose a different perspective

The normal tendency is to take a picture either from your phone or camera at eye level. But if you want to create a fresh viewpoint on your photos, I encourage you to experiment with different angles. Consider taking above or below shots. If you have a great camera, you could even take low to the ground shots without having to crouch or lay down on the floor.

Draw the viewer's eye

This is something I learned from a professional photographer. He taught me the concept of "leading lines." These are lines that run through an image that draws the eye and add a sense of depth. You can use this technique to add motion or purpose to your photo. Roads, buildings, and natural elements such as waves, trees, waterfalls help create this effect, so always keep an eye out for the possibility of adding this to your photo when shooting. Another way to add depth is by including layers or using objects in the background and the foreground.

With that basic understanding of the principles involved in good photography, I would like to share some of the subjects and themes that perform well on Instagram.

#1. Symmetry

Anything symmetrical will always be pleasing to the eye. Whether you're taking a picture in nature or a man-made product, focus on creating symmetry, and you can't go wrong.

#2. Vibrant colors

There are lots of awesome Instagram profiles that go against the trend and produce content with rich, bold, and bright colors. If you can capture this high energy and vibrancy in a still picture (don't worry, there are editing tools to give you that extra punch), even a mundane picture can look absolutely stunning.

#3. Patterns

Our brains love patterns, so if you can capture beautiful patterns in your pictures, you can do really well. Look around you in nature and architecture to find patterns that you can share with your audience.

#4. Captivating background

A still picture on a stunning background will almost always look gorgeous when done right. This is an easy one to do, whether it's for a product or a selfie. Find or create an epic background, and it will transform the final look of your picture.

#5. Detail shots

Still pictures can become attention-grabbing on your feed if you place a sharp focus on an unexpected or interesting detail. I find these photos very calming and cleansing to the eye, especially after scrolling through a noisy feed. Instagram has editing tools like vignettes or tile shit, which enhance details and specific areas of a photo. If you want to get a nice still shot with this level of detail, I recommend taking it in close range, so the quality remains intact.

Once you decide which set up and direction works for your photoshoot, experiment with some of these ideas and let your creativity guide you into that perfect shot.

USING FILTERS IN YOUR PICTURES

I mentioned the use of filters such as Vignette, and if you're new to this, you might be wondering what filters are and why we need them. Remember the anecdote I made earlier about the sun having a natural filter when it's low on the horizon that makes everything look more beautiful? If you test it out today by going out and taking a photo just before sunset and then again during sunset, you'll see what I mean. There's an added effect that makes the whole experience stunning. Instagram, as well as other editing software tools, have the same ability to "unnaturally" adjust and modify the look and feel of your photo. Instagram comes with in-built filters that you can use to manipulate your photo's final look before publishing. By using one to three of the same filters throughout your feed, a harmonious effect is created. All the big accounts you follow, especially from beauty celebrities and fashionistas, have this in common. They all use certain filters consistently. Even the food blogger that makes you swoon each time a new post shows up is most likely using a carefully picked out filter. As part of creating a brand identity and a consistent experience, it's your turn to choose a filter that you can start testing for your feed.

The top and most popular filters on Instagram if you don't wish to use an external app are Clarendon, Gingham, and Juno.

Clarendon brightens, highlights, and enhances your photo with one tap. It intensifies shadows and makes colors pop, making it very multi-purpose, so it's not surprising that it's the number one choice for many Instagrammers.

Gingham has a vintage feel to it and brightens warm hues making an image appear rich and authentic.

Juno adds saturation, warmth, and a bit of punch to colors, making it a great all-purpose filter.

Aside from these filters, you also have Lark, Valencia, Mayfair, Rise, Amaro, Earlybird, Aden, and X-Pro II filter ranking as top filters to use on Instagram. The most important thing to remember is that you cannot overuse these filters or pick too many on your feed. If you want to see big brands using filters exceptionally well, I encourage you to check out Lululemon, Sephora, and HubSpot. These may not be in your niche, but they will give you some inspiration on how to go about choosing your filters.

Decide whether you're going for a warm & rustic feel, clean & crisp, or dark and moody feed. That will give you some guidance and help you rule out many of the filters to focus on the ones that match your feed's mood. Remember to check with your brand identity and make sure the choices align and help represent you well. The main intention here is to connect your audience to a particular emotion. Please note that you'll also have the option of adding filters when it comes to Instagram Stories. We'll discuss that when sharing hacks to crush it with Instagram Stories. So even if you want to play around with multiple filters, you can do so on your Stories. If, however, you want something more than what

Instagram offers by default, you can download apps to help with your photo editing.

PHOTO EDITING APPS TO MAKE YOUR PICTURES STUNNING:

Need to add some visual flair and effects that go beyond the basics that Instagram offers? Although I think Instagram already provides tons of useful functionality, here are apps that can help you do the trick even if you have no photography or graphics background.

VSCO for Android and iOS

Over 200 million Instagram posts feature the #VSCO, which tells me this is a super popular photo editing tool. With this tool, you get about ten free pre-set filters that can enhance your photo. You also get lots of other tools to manipulate things like contrast, saturation, intensity, and so on. You can also crop your picture on the app. If you want more robust features, you can always upgrade to open up over 200 filters and other features.

A Color Story for Android and iOS

The app seems to be specializing in making colors pop in your photos. It's simple to use and comes with 20 free editing tools, including filters, effects, and pre-sets designed by professional photographers and influencers.

Adobe Lightroom Photo Editor for Android and iOS

Adobe products all have powerful capabilities, and this photo editor is no exception. You can edit raw images and turn your mobile shot pictures into high quality, professional-looking photos that look like they were shot on film. The app allows you to manipulate hues, saturation, exposure, shadows, and so much more. It also comes with some pre-set filters that are great for those who don't want to get into the nitty-gritty of editing.

Snapseed for Android and iOS

This app is especially useful for professional or amateur photographers. It allows you to work on both JPG and RAW files with as much detail as you like and goes beyond the standard touch-ups the rest of us like to use. Yes, it comes with pre-sets but what's great about this app is the serious photo editing skills you could do thanks to the 29 tools and features that come with the app. You can even remove elements (including people) from your photo or adjust the geometry of buildings. And all that with incredible precision and quality.

Instagram Layout for Android and iOS

This layout from the Instagram app is free and allows you to compile up to nine photos in various combinations. It makes it easy to design and layout, especially if you want to create collages. You can add filters and other personalized elements to quickly share on Instagram.

Lipix app for Android and iOS

It is another great photo collage and picture editor which allows you to combine up to nine photos into a single frame. You can personalize and customize it with stickers and texts and easily share it on Instagram.

Canva

Canva is a highly popular graphics designing software with both free and pro versions. Even if you have no design skills, this web-based software will help you create amazing photos with tons of filters and pre-made templates. They also have a mobile app for Insta Stories that allows you to create content for your Instagram Stories fast, just like the pros.

SAVING DRAFTS

Once you've created your awesome picture, you may not want to publish it just yet for whatever reason. During those times, you can take advantage of Instagram's draft functionality, which allows you to save the post and publish it later. Tap the camera icon at the top of your screen to create the post, then take or upload your photo and click Next. Here you can add effects, filters, a caption, or your location. To save this post without publishing, you need to go back to the filtering and editing step, then tap the back arrow in the top left corner > Save Draft. You can only save it as a draft after editing the post and adding your captions, location, etc. In other words, it needs to be ready for publication before you can save it as a draft. If you want to access your posts, tap the camera icon again, then find Library or Gallery, and you should be able to see them.

If you want to tidy up your drafts section and discard unnecessary posts, make your way back to the drafts section and tap on select all, then tap the edit button. Tap the saved posts you want to delete and hit the discard posts button.

POSTING AND SHARING FROM MOBILE AND DESKTOP

We already know Instagram is a mobile-first app. Most of its features have been built so that you either take a picture from your mobile phone or upload it and instantly publish it to your feed. The process is pretty straightforward. It guides you through the editing steps, adding captions, tagging people, adding your location, and even posting on other connected platforms such as your Facebook page. Once you hit publish, the post appears on your feed.

And while this is fast and convenient, many creators, including myself, have been looking for ways to post from a desktop. When you want to use more advanced tools and equipment, learning simple tricks that enable you to upload edited pictures from your desktop can be a time and energy saver. Here's how you can do it.

A quick hack for posting from your desktop:

For this example, I am using a Mac desktop because it's what I use. First, you need to log into your Instagram account through Google Chrome. Once you're in your account, click on "View" on the top-most ribbon of your computer screen (where your clock is) for a drop-down menu. Then, go to Developer > Developer Tools. A sidebar should open up on your screen, showing you the code of the Instagram webpage. From there, click on "Toggle device bar," which is an icon that shows a phone and a bigger device (next to "Elements"). Next, you should notice a little ribbon on the right part of your screen (next to the developer sidebar) with a drop-down menu set to "Responsive." Click on that and change the setting to be your preference – like iPhone X. You should see the Instagram layout change to match the setting you selected, with the camera + icon at the bottom of the Instagram screen for uploading a post. If this does not appear automatically, try refreshing your page. You can operate the Instagram page as usual. You're all set.

That's a fast way that costs you no money. Still, if you want to find alternatives, you can always sign up for third-party tools like Hootsuite, Later, CoSchedule, and Buffer, which all perform the same task.

CURATING AND REPOSTING CONTENT FROM OTHER INSTAGRAM ACCOUNTS:

You can easily curate content from other accounts. All you need is the account owner's permission in writing and either an app or the weblink I will be walking you through shortly. To get permission, consider either leaving a message on the comment box or sending a direct message with your request. I also encourage you to tag and mention the original source of your content whenever you repost something.

You have a variety of options, most of which are free when it comes to regramming awesome content. In some cases, you might need to download an app from your Google Play or Apple store.

#1. DownloadGram

The first option is to use this weblink that lets you download high-resolution copies of Instagram photos and videos to repost on your account. I like this option because you don't even need to download any additional app to make it work. Just follow these simple steps.

First, open your Instagram and find the photo or video you want to repost, then tap the ••icon in the upper righthand corner of the post. Click "Copy Share URL."

Second, paste the URL into the DownloadGram, which can be accessed through your mobile internet browser at www. downloadgram.com, then tap "Download." Scroll to the bottom of the homepage and click "Download Image," and you'll be directed to a new webpage with the content ready to download. Tap the download icon, then "Save Image."

Third, head over to your Instagram and upload as you would a normal image. It should be automatically stored in your camera images so just follow the normal steps of editing, adding tags, captions, etc., before reposting.

#2. Taking Screenshots

You can also repost using the simple method of taking a screenshot of a photo you like on Instagram. For iOS, you need to press down on the home and lock buttons simultaneously until the screen flashes. For Android, you need to press down on the sleep/wake and volume down buttons simultaneously until the screen flashes.

Then head over to your Instagram and tap the camera + icon. Resize the photo and edit it to fit the Instagram size. In this case, I also encourage you to tag and include the user-name of the original creator.

#3. Repost for Instagram for iOS and Android

This is a free app that integrates directly with Instagram that lets you curate and share content right from your mobile device. To use it, simply download the app. Then open Instagram, tap the ••icon on the upper right corner, and choose "Copy Share URL."

Open Repost and then go back to your Instagram to find the image you want. Copy the specific post URL you'd like to share to your clipboard. Then, head back to repost, where the copied post should automatically appear on the home-page. Tap the arrow on the right-hand side of the post. If you want to edit or make adjustments, this is where you do it. Once you're happy with the image, tap "Repost." Then tap "Copy to Instagram," where you can add a filter and edit the post. Remember to edit the post captions before sharing your repost.

8

CREATING AWESOME VIDEOS FOR INSTAGRAM

*J*ust because you shoot videos for YouTube or Facebook doesn't mean you can automatically upload them on Instagram. The platform isn't designed for long-form content and since we know it's a visual-based image first platform, experimenting with videos is an excellent idea if we add a bit of flair that aligns with the demands of the platforms. In this section of the book, we will walk through the process of creating or even repurposing videos that attract and drive engagement to your profile.

There are several ways you can experiment with videos. First, you can upload the video on your feed as you do a regular still image. There is a limit on the size and length of this, which we'll discuss shortly. The second option is to publish Instagram Stories, which have become extremely popular. The third option is to create Instagram reels. Last but not least, it is to create your own IG TV library. Let's start with the most popular option – Instagram Stories.

INSTAGRAM STORIES

What is Instagram Story? An Instagram story is a photo or video that you create and share, which is visible to your followers and to users you follow. Instagram Stories are unique in that they disappear after 24hrs just like with Snapchat. It is published separately from your feeds' gallery, although you can highlight them in the "Highlights" section of your account.

To create an Instagram Story, open your Instagram app, and click your profile picture at the screen's bottom right. Then click the big plus + icon at the top right corner of the screen, which will open up a drop-down menu where you can select the "Story" option (second option from the top under Create New). You can also start a Story by clicking on the +icon that appears right next to your image while viewing the "Home" dashboard.

You have the ability to share an existing image or video by swiping up, which will take you into your phone's camera. If you want to create something in-the-moment, you can choose the "Lens" icon, which lets you do several things:

- Create – this is the first option you'll see. It enables you to type text on a plain background without a photo.

- Layout – this option lets you take several different pictures to make a collage (up to six depending on the layout you choose). You can also upload images from your camera.

- Live – this option lets you broadcast live on the Instagram platform. Similar to Facebook Live, your friends and followers can interact with you. Once your broadcast is over, you can allow it to run its course and disappear, you can save it, or you can publish on Instagram Stories, where it can be accessed for an additional 24hrs.

- Normal – this option lets you either capture a still image (tap once) or record a video (press and hold it down).

- Boomerang – this option films looping GIFs up to three seconds long. These ones are simple, fun, and get lots of attention when done right.

- Superzoom – this is a video recording lens that zooms in closer and closer on your subject. It comes with different filters that produce various effects such as fire, heart, and so fun. These can be really fun to play with.

- Handsfree – this option works like a timer on a

camera. Use it when you want it to film for you but just make sure the subject is ready and that your phone is set somewhere stable like on a tripod.

- Reels – this option lets you take short little videos that you clip together. You can add music and filters.

How To View Instagram Stories

Instagram Stories all appear at the top of your screen when on the mobile app. They are positioned in such a way that users have to see these first, which means they get a ton of engagement. That's why doing more Instagram Stories can help you grow your followers fast. To view someone's Instagram story, you need to open your app and tap the home icon on the bottom left-hand corner of your screen. Once there, you'll see a series of circular icons along the top, each of which represents the active Stories posted by the users you follow. Tap on the circular icon to view a user's Story. A single Instagram Story can contain numerous individual photos and videos strung together in the order they were posted, starting with the newest. Swipe left or right to navigate between Stories from different users. If you're viewing an ad, swiping up will allow you to head over to the link the user wants you to view.

THE BEST CONTENT FOR INSTAGRAM STORIES

#1. Product explainer or demo

You don't need to have the sexiest or simplest product to make this work. With a bit of creativity and personality, you can create short, quirky videos demonstrating your product. Instagram is the perfect format for showing potential customers how your product is used and the benefits. Create a video that's segmented into 15-second clips to walk users through your product or even a service you offer and show them how their lives can improve. If humor is your thing, then add a few doses of that as well.

#2. Give shout-outs to other business or influencers

This is a great way to passively nurture relationships with users that matter most to your brand. You can create Stories on a product you use that you'd love to partner with or praise an influencer for their latest review if you want to promote that influencer to your audience so you can eventually build a mutually beneficial connection. You can also create shout-outs to certain customers (with their permission). This will encourage them to promote your account because everyone likes to be praised on social media.

#3. Preview your blogs or Vlogs

If you are currently blogging on your website or Vlogging on YouTube, this is a great way to give your content more exposure. You can help Instagram users discover your awesome content for the first time. I've seen Google do this on their feed whereby they preview an article on their Instagram Story. At the end of the Story, Google prompts you to swipe up with your finger where you're sent over to the link with the full blog post.

#4. Share a day-in-the-life-of

This is something I have seen many Instagrammers do at some point during their journey. They document for an entire day how they spend their day, where they work, what it's like to be an Instagrammer, and so on. People love watching these types of stories. You'll need to plan it out beforehand and figure out how you will segment this and the different aspects of your day that you can share. It can be a lot of fun, and it creates a strong connection with your audience.

#5. Promote an event

You can create a series promoting an upcoming event you're hosting online or offline. You can also promote a conference or seminar you will be attending even if you're not the host. People love seeing where you're going, and the cool people you get to meet. This is also beneficial to you because if you add the event hashtags, your Stories can be discovered by attendees of the event, which gives your profile more exposure and new followers. When promoting an event, always remember to add the event name and official hashtag.

TRICKS AND HACKS FOR YOUR INSTAGRAM STORIES

Add your brand colors and fonts to your Stories

There's a ton of fun fonts, and it's great to play around with different colors and fonts. But if you want to train your audience to recognize your brand, it's vital to focus more on using the fonts and brands you chose earlier in this book. To have your own customized fonts, you will need to download the app Over mobile. Once you download, AirDrop your fonts.OFT file into your mobile device. Follow the simple instructions that follow, and once it's done, you'll be able to incorporate brand fonts into your Stories.

Turn Live Photos into Boomerangs

You can turn a live photo into a Boomerang, but the live image needs to be taken within the last 24hours. To do this, simply open Instagram Stories, swipe up, and pick a live photo from your camera roll. Once you find the image you want, press firmly on the screen for a few seconds until you see the word "Boomerang" appear briefly. And that's it! You just made a new Boomerang that you can share.

Copy a Photo from your Camera Roll

By hitting the "Copy" option from an image in your camera roll and adding it to an Instagram Story you're creating, you can add an extra photo of Gif as long as you're using the "Create" option of your Instagram Stories. It makes you post funkier, so have fun with this.

Track Best Performers

It's essential to keep track of the content that is getting you the most engagement, especially reshares. Unfortunately, you won't find this data in the regular insights section. Instead, you need to tap the ellipsis in the top right corner of a post to pull up a menu with the option to "View Story Reshares." This will show you all the current posts that are being reshared. If you don't see anything, then it's likely that none is being reshared. When promoting an event or a sale, this particular hack is handy because it helps you get user-generated content and shows you how people react.

IGTV

Since its launch in 2018, IGTV (Instagram TV) has gained momentum and popularity amongst creators. At first, it was only supporting vertical videos, but today it can support both vertical and horizontal videos that are up to ten minutes long for regular accounts. Certified accounts (with the blue tick) get even more playtime on IGTV.

As a beginner, you can use those ten minutes to create incredible content that can boost your engagement levels, especially with the right content planning. IGTV videos can also be previewed right from your main profile feed, making it easy for new or existing followers to watch your videos. You'll have to turn on the toggle that enables this functionality before publishing the video on IGTV. You and your audience can watch IGTV videos in the Instagram app, in the standalone IGTV app, or by clicking the IGTV icon accessible on the explore/discovery page. You can also click on the IGTV button on your profile or someone else's Instagram profile. When you post a new IGTV video, your followers will get a notification in the native Instagram app.

How to set up your IGTV

As long as you have an Instagram account, you can immediately start your Instagram TV because the feature is now fully integrated into their main platform. To upload an IGTV video, which can be a maximum of fifteen minutes long, open the Instagram app, and tap the search icon (looks like a magnifying glass) at the bottom of your screen. This will bring you to the discovery page, where you will see the

IGTV icon right next to the shop icon. Click on the IGTV icon, and that will bring you to a new area specifically dedicated to IGTV content. You will see a Plus + icon on the upper right-hand corner, which, when clicked, will open up your video library. Choose the video you wish to upload, then click "Next." Here you can add a cover by uploading a pre-made one from your gallery or simply sticking with the default that the app generates automatically. Click "Next" and add a title and description. This is also where you can switch on the ability to post a preview on your feed and profile. You could also make it visible on Facebook if you've linked your accounts.

If the video is part of a series of content, you're creating IGTV gives you the ability to group them into a series that people can watch chronologically. This is wonderful for educational content and how-to tutorials. Once you're ready to publish, click post and give it a few minutes for the video to be distributed on the platform.

The best file format on IGTV is always MP4 with a video length between 1 minute and 15 minutes long. The maximum length you can upload if your account qualifies is 1 hour. Go for a vertical aspect ratio of 9:16 or a horizontal aspect ratio of 16:9. The minimum recommended resolution is 720 pixels and a minimum frame rate of 30 frames per second. The best cover photo size is a ratio of 1:1.55 or 420 px by 654 px. When it comes to file size for videos that are 10 minutes or less, Instagram recommends a maximum of 650MB. For videos up to 60 minutes long, the maximum file size should never exceed 3.6GB.

TYPES OF CONTENT THAT PERFORM WELL ON IGTV

Tutorial Videos

How-to videos that cover a variety of topics in your niche can build lots of engagement. For example, if you're a fitness influencer, you could create a series focused on home-based workouts without equipment.

Educational content

You can create fun, colorful educational content teaching your audience about something relevant to them. Take inspiration from Bulletproof's IGTV. They make videos explaining their ingredients, how they source them, and some of the more technical terms used in their products. Even if you're not a big supplement company like Bulletproof, you can still create something engaging using well-designed slideshows to educate your audience.

Showcase and behind the scenes content

A great inspiration you can definitely see for showcasing real estate is with Rob Report. They regularly publish videos showcasing incredible listings. You can give people a full tour of the home if you're in real estate. You could also give people a behind-the-scenes look if you work in a studio or have something working in the background that your audience usually doesn't get to see.

The most important thing to remember is that you need to create content that suits your brand and enriches your audience's lives. Go deeper with your content, get creative, and focus on adding value.

TIPS TO MAKE YOUR IGTV SUCCESSFUL

Focus on quality

Although you need to consistently create lots of content, I think it's better to create good quality and engaging content that massive volumes of meaningless content. Play the long game and let your audience learn to trust your quality and the effort you put into these videos. That will drive more engagement as your account grows.

Design clear custom covers

Invest some time creating customized custom covers that are clear and communicate the main message. The optimum cover size, as mentioned earlier, is 420 by 654 pixels. Use a tool such as Canva, which already comes with pre-made templates and properly sized graphics that you can easily plug and play with.

Add a link to your IGTV video

Instagram has added lots of new features since 2010, but URLs are still a struggle for us as there aren't many places to add a link unless you have lots of followers. Fortunately, IGTV allows you to insert a clickable link in the video description. You can link to a website, a freebie, or your shop so take advantage of this feature.

RECORDING VIDEOS

Recording your videos on Instagram is pretty straightforward. Open up your Instagram app and head over to the top left corner of the screen, where you should see the Camera + icon. To upload a video from your phone's library, select the video you'd like to share. If you want to record on the go, tap the camera icon above your phone's library, then tap and hold on the circular record icon. Lift your finger to stop recording.

Like taking great pictures, you need to focus on having great lighting if you want to record quality videos. Keep a focus on one subject as much as you can and keep the shot steady. Consider using a tripod or stacks of books. Instagram now accepts both vertical and horizontal videos. Still, for beginners, I always encourage landscape unless it's for Instagram Stories Videos.

BEFORE YOU POST

Now that you have your video ready to share with the world, I recommend adding a bit of flair to it through editing to make it pop. There are a few handy apps that you can use even if you're a complete amateur.

Boomerang

The boomerang feature comes in-built on the app and allows you to create bite-sized videos, almost like GIFs. It can be a quick fun way to create a video on the go.

A Color Story

This app works for both iOS and Android and is all about filters. There are over three hundred filters, both free and paid. It quickly enhances the color and aesthetics of your videos and saves your edits as filters so you can apply the same look to the other videos.

Animoto

This app works with both iOS and Android and focuses more on creating epic slideshows. If you have several photos or videos you want to put together, this is the way to go. The free version works when creating videos of up to ten minutes.

Inshot

This video editing app is considered one of the best. It trims clips, changes footage speed, adds filters and texts, zooms in and out, and even lets you incorporate your own music. The interface is super simple to use. Almost anyone can quickly turn their video into something that stands out on Instagram.

LIVESTREAMING ON INSTAGRAM

You can do up to one hour of live video broadcasting on Instagram. Once the broadcast is done, you can either share the replay on your IGTV or put it on Live Archive to share later. To go live, tap the camera icon in the top left of your feed and scroll to Live at the bottom of the screen. Then tap the record icon. If you have viewers joining live, you should see the number count at the top of the screen. Your viewers can interact with you during the broadcast. All comments appear at the bottom of the screen, and if you want to add your comment, Instagram has that feature included; just tap the "Comment" icon. If you'd like to Pin a particular comment, such as a link for your call-to-action, tap that comment and then tap "Pin Comment" so that all viewers can see it more easily. At the end of the Livestreaming, remember to tap "End" in the top right corner and then tap the download icon in the top left if you want to save it to your camera roll or share it on IGTV.

REELS

Reels are a new way to create and discover short, entertaining videos on Instagram. You can record and edit 15-second multi-clip videos with audio effects and so much more and then share with your followers and the entire Instagram community because they show up on the Explore page. For business accounts, reels are a fantastic new way to be discovered by new users. If you use original sounds and hashtags, there's a chance you might go viral if people like the effects on your reel. Users also have the ability to use your audio when they select "Use Audio" from your reel.

You can post your reel on your regular profile feed where it will remain visible, or you can create a Story reel that will disappear after 24hrs.

Given that this is one of the newer features Instagram added at the end of 2020, I expect they will give content creators with great reels a lot more reach to promote this feature, so get creative and start making your reels.

To make your first reel, click on the "movie reel" icon that now shows up at the bottom of the screen. Here you will have various editing tools, including Audio, AR effects, Timer and countdown, Align, and Speed.

- AR Effects - you get an abundance of effects to choose from created by both Instagram and creators worldwide.
- Audio - opens up a music library. Here you can choose from one of the pre-existing tracks or use your own original audio.
- Align - line up objects from your previous clip before recording your next clip that way, you can have a seamless transition.
- Timer and Countdown - set a timer so you can record any of your clips hands-free.

If Instagram loves your reel, they can tag it with a "Featured" label, which will drive massive attention across the platform, making it an incredible way to get more traffic to your profile and brand.

SECTION 04: MANAGING YOUR INSTAGRAM ACCOUNT

9

THE BEST PRACTICES ON MANAGING AN INSTAGRAM ACCOUNT

*N*ow that your account is up and running, your job is to maintain it until you have enough momentum to create a snowball effect. Ever heard of Instagrammers who speak of overnight success with their accounts? Chances are, they were really consistent for a prolonged time period, and then one day, all that effort snowballed into spectacular results. So, the main focus, once you're up and running, is to create structures that enable you to keep attracting new customers.

To do this, you need a tool that can help you analyze your success, learn more about your audience, and repeat more of what's working. While many social listening tools provide all this data for you, e.g., Iconosquare and Socialbakers, feel free to begin small if you don't have the budget.

DEVELOP A DAILY TO-DO LIST

Whether you're doing this full time or as a side hustle after work, you need a daily list of things that must be done to ensure the growth of your account and brand. Always have a content calendar to work from so you can know what content to create and publish. I encourage you to have days scheduled for content creation and other days for community engagement. If you're using scheduling tools such as Buffer or Later to push out content, this will save you time so that you can invest it elsewhere, such as creating more content or editing your videos.

Don't make your daily to-do list impossible to accomplish. A list of three things done daily and efficiently will yield better results than have too much to do, leading to procrastination.

For example, you can have a daily task of investing 30min exploring accounts posting the same hashtags you use so you can develop that connection. You can also create one piece of content daily. However, you choose to organize yourself, make sure it's not overwhelming, and that it can be done based on the time commitment you give yourself. Reflect on your current lifestyle before determining your daily list.

ANALYZING YOUR INSTAGRAM

If you want to grow your brand and account, you'll have to track and measure everything. That's the only way to know what works and what doesn't. Luckily, Instagram already offers that data for each post under your "Insights" tab. Go to your main profile dashboard, and you will see three tabs (Promotions Insights Contact). By clicking on Insights, you can instantly navigate between a summary or in-depth view of your account to see performance, content interactions, and followers. You can see the last 7 days and the breakdown of the content you shared on the feed, IGTV, and Stories.

Suppose you're working on a campaign with a specific objective. In that case, I suggest you do some A/B testing to figure out what works best so you can adjust your strategy. A few things to keep in mind when running A/B tests is that you must choose a single element to test. So that can be an image, caption, hashtag, etc. Do not test multiple things at the same time. Create a variation based on the same content except for that single element being tested and then track and analyze each post's results. The one that performs best is what you should create more of. If you want to further experiment and optimize, you can take the winning content and adjust another new element, then test to find a new winner. Rinse and repeat this formula. Have a spreadsheet where all this data is collected if you want optimum results.

DEALING WITH HATERS

Let's not kid ourselves; as your brand and Instagram accounts continue to grow with raving fans, you're also going to bump into a lot more haters. The trolls of the Internet are plentiful and eagerly awaiting your debut. Many people have more courage to hate on people while hiding behind a computer and fake usernames. So be forewarned, the success that awaits you will also bring with it some of these unpleasant trolls who enjoy criticizing and hating on all your hard work. It can sometimes feel very discouraging to find a mean comment on your feed, so how do you deal with this?

#1: Remember these are just insecure bullies

Even in school, the people who like to hurt others are usually projecting their personal hurt and insecurities. Think of trolls the same way. The fact that someone consumed your content and took time to leave a mean comment means you must have had some impact on them. But due to their insecurities, they were unable to express themselves in the right way, so you triggered a nerve. That hater is just showing you how much he or she wishes they had or could do what you just demonstrated. Keep that in mind the next time you find a mean comment, and instead of lashing out, just keep scrolling and attending to your fans.

#2: Let your raving fans deal with haters.

If you already have an engaged community with active followers who love your content, just hand over your trolls to your tribe and watch them eat them alive. I have seen this a lot with people like Gary Vee or Grant Cardone, who often get haters. What do they do? They turn it around to their community, and as for their input. The reaction is usually massive as their fans attack the troll and almost bury him in defense of their beloved guru. Now, you may not yet have that much influence, but it's something to look forward to.

#3: Give kindness instead

If you are a spiritual or religious person, then this should make sense. Kindness given to someone who doesn't deserve it can be very liberating to the one who gives. It's not always easy, but if you can find it in you to reply with a kind word, I encourage you to do so. Don't fake or force it. It needs to come from a place of authentic kindness and compassion. Develop the understanding that human beings are inherently good. Some of us are just raised poorly, or we've just endured way too many bad days.

HOW TO AVOID GETTING BANNED AND WHAT TO DO IF YOU GET SHADOWBANNED BY INSTAGRAM

As you grow your account, you might experience issues with your content reach for various reasons. Instagram is constantly changing its algorithm, so it is essential to keep reviewing their terms and new updates. As long as you avoid doing things that could get you banned, such as overusing hashtags, buying followers, and using bots, you should be fine. If, however, you still think your content isn't getting as much reach as it deserves, it could be that Instagram is shadowbanning your content. Although they don't openly admit to doing this, they did release a report stating that some business accounts reported the issue and recommend focusing on putting out great content instead of hashtag stuffing. According to Instagram, the best way to grow and get your content seen by more people who don't follow you is to create something thoughtful and appealing to the Instagram community. It's not about trying to manipulate the system.

With that said, if you want to be sure that Instagram isn't shadowbanning you, here's a simple test. Post content with a single hashtag that isn't often used. Don't go for something with millions of followers because you won't know if your content is banned or hidden by competition. Once posted, get five people who don't follow you to search the hashtag. If none of them see your post in those results, you've likely been shadowbanned.

Now, the main reason you can get banned, as I just mentioned, is due to the tactics you've been using to grow the account. Instagram frowns on tools that shortcut your growth, such as bots, so review what you're currently using. If you are using anything, Instagram considers spammy, stop it immediately. The other reason could be that you're overusing hashtags or that you're using broken hashtags that aren't relevant to your topic. It could also be that users report your account as spammy or inappropriate several times. This might lead to Instagram disabling your account or shadowbanning you. That's why I have been insisting on targeting an audience that is narrow enough so that you can be confident they care about your content and topics.

One last tip I can give you is to regularly go through the list of banned hashtags to make sure what you use aligns with Instagram's terms of use. The best way to figure out which hashtags are banned is to go to the "Explore" tab and search the hashtag. If nothing appears, it's likely banned either temporarily or forever. You can also check on Instagram's hashtag page, where they post new updates. Examples of banned hashtags that you must never use include #assday #curvygirls #petitie #alone #bikinibody #date #dating

#humpday #killingit #kissing #mustfollow #pornfood #singlelife #stranger #shit #teens #thighs #undies etc.

TOOLS FOR MANAGING YOUR ACCOUNT

Some of the tools you will need to manage your account have already been mentioned. A tool like Instagram Insights, which comes in-built as long as you have a business account, is excellent. If you prefer a third-party tool that's easy to use, you can opt for Later, Hootsuite, or Buffer, all of which have both free and paid versions. If, however you'd like to explore more analytical tools, consider getting Iconosquare (specializes in social monitoring), Crowdfire (specializes in content curation), Pixlee (for social reports), Union Metrics (for hashtags analytics, Socialbakers (for competitive analysis) especially if you want to compare how your account is doing relative to peers in the same niche.

10

GAINING FOLLOWERS

To get the most out of your Instagram and reach your business objectives, gaining followers is the defining factor. If you don't get attention and convert that attention into followers, fans, and buyers, all this effort is in vain. Instagram is a social platform where you need to show people you are a real human being who cares about engaging with others. You must remain active outside set posting times. You also need to follow other people if you want others to follow you. Nowadays, it's not enough to post content and use hashtags, so here are the various ways you can get real people who care about and engage with your brand.

Like and comment on top accounts

This is one of the most effective ways to build engagement on your account and have new people discover your brand. It requires time investment because you need to find and interact with accounts that you believe your users interact with as well. Apply everything you've learned so far and getting to know which accounts to interact with won't be too hard. For example, if there's a hashtag that your users typically search for, you can visit it daily to find the top-ranked posts and leave a comment on the content that most resonates with you. That can lead the account owner and the other users coming over to your account and liking your content as well. It's a natural way of creating reciprocity and could lead to new followers, especially if you target the right hashtags.

Respond to comments

This should be common sense, but unfortunately, common sense isn't always common practice. Always respond to all the comments on your post. The more people see you engaging with users who take the time to comment on your posts, the more likely they are to engage with you as well because they see you genuinely care about socializing. I know it's easy to find big brands with lots of comments that they never respond to but don't use that as a standard policy for your brand if you want to gain followers. Human to human social interaction is what Instagram is all about.

Until you become too big with too many followers to respond to, take time daily to reply in the comments section.

Reply to Direct Messages

Besides responding to people when they leave a comment, you should also reply to any DM (direct messages) that land on your Instagram inbox. Although the public doesn't see this interaction, it can help you grow your brand credibility. Another neat trick is to initiate communication via direct messages. Regularly let people know on your Stories or Feed that you usually offer some goodies via direct messages. That will encourage people to want to follow and interact with you in this personalized way.

User-generated Content

This type of content is created by existing customers and fans. They can create shout-outs for you or short videos demonstrating or explaining how they've used and benefited from your product or service. This type of content is absolutely phenomenal because it sells for you. People love to get the assurance that purchasing your product is risk-free and that it will improve their lives. The more of this content you can push out to the platform, the likely you are to attract potential buyers who will, of course, follow and interact more keenly with your brand.

Run a contest on Instagram

Giveaways and contests are huge on Instagram and can be a great source of follower acquisition. Plan it right and make the criteria for participating tagging a friend. You're likely to see a spike in your follower count. Just make sure the reward is exciting enough for the existing and potential followers you wish to attract.

Collaborating with Influencers

This is a strategy I used years ago, and it grew my account overnight. I know I'm not the only one who has experienced success with leveraging influencers. The trick is to build a strong relationship with the right influencer. If you work with the right influencer and come up with a mutually beneficial strategy, getting that exposure to his or her audience will lead to an increase in the number of followers who choose to continue consuming your content. The most important thing is to create high-value content and build a real connection with both the influencer and his or her audience.

Get the blue tick aka a verified badge

Getting verified by Instagram can actually help you gain more followers because when people see that blue tick next to your name, it automatically makes them assume you're a big deal. People always love to follow important-looking accounts. Although anyone can request the badge, there are specific requirements Instagram demands. I suggest reading their terms before making the request. If you feel you qualify, then open your Instagram app, tap your profile picture in the bottom right to go to your profile. Click on the three parallel bars in the top right, then tap Settings. Tap Account, then tap Request Verification. You will need to provide your details, including your full name and some form of identification.

Having this verification badge will exponentially increase the number of followers because you'll be considered authoritative and newsworthy. However, I don't recommend you attempt to request it until you get 5,000 followers.

Promote your account

It's time to think outside the Instagram box so you can bring more followers to your brand. Consider leveraging other social networks such as Facebook, YouTube, Twitter, Pinterest, and LinkedIn to drive traffic to your Instagram profile. You can also include your Instagram icon in the footer of your emails or as part of your signature and ask people to connect with you there. If you have a blog or website, consider embedding your Instagram feed to entice that audience to join you on Instagram. There are free plugins like Smash Balloon that make it easy to add a widget even if you're not tech-savvy. Be creative with this and how you choose to cross-promote and repurpose your content across the web.

11

USING INSTAGRAM FOR BUSINESS

With an Instagram business account, you not only have access to audience insight, but you can also conduct a lot of business to generate sales. Instagram just integrated the "Instagram Shop" tab across the platform, making it easier and faster than ever for your followers to turn into buying customers. You can access the shop from the main profile feed by clicking on your profile picture. It's one of the main three tabs right next to Promotions and Insights. Here you can tag products in your posts or story, showcase your products in a customizable way creating your very own storefront, and even get insights about how your shop is performing.

Here are some helpful tips to ensure you get the most from your business account.

Take advantage of the new features.

Add a Shop to your Instagram profile and also include contact information, category, and some calls to action so that users can know about your offer, how to get it and how to connect with you.

Create Instagram Guides

Depending on the niche you serve you can create motivational guides using posts, product guides to showcase your best offers (just make sure they are the ones included in your Instagram Shop) and you can even create guides for your city to offer helpful recommendations if you've got a brick-and-mortar business.

Link your shop to your Instagram Story

This is also a new feature that lets you link back to your shop with every Instagram story you create. Doing business has never been easier whether you sell a product or service.

Build anticipation and offer exclusive deals through your Instagram Stories and Instagram Live broadcasts.

This is a great way to get your audience excited about something new. It's also a nice reward for your new followers. Do you have a lead magnet that can lead to the latest product?

Why not offer it exclusively to all new followers within a given timeframe. Create teaser photos and Stories, letting people know how they can receive your freebie and get their hands on your latest offer.

Run Instagram Ads

Instagram ads are sponsored content that allow you to reach a broader audience by paying Facebook (the parent company). They are currently among the cheapest form of online advertising. Yet, the return on investment can be huge if you have a strong paid ads strategy. I like Instagram ads because you don't need a big budget to get started. With Instagram Stories ads, you could be spending less than $5 a day and getting a lot of traffic to your profile or landing page. All Instagram ads have a "Sponsored" tag on them. You can run Stories ads, Photo ads, Video ads, Carousel ads, Collection ads, Explore ads, IGTV ads, and Instagram Shopping ads. Each ad type works differently depending on your business goals. The most important thing to know is what objective you are aiming for and how much you are willing to spend.

SHOULD YOU HIRE A SOCIAL MEDIA MANAGER OR WORK WITH AN AGENCY?

Most people assume social media marketing for business is as easy as social media for personal use. Unfortunately, this is far from the truth. Marketing a brand online requires discipline, planning, and significant knowledge of the best practices and trends. That is where a social media manager comes in. He or she gathers metrics on page performance, engagement, and followers, sets goals, focuses on branding and brand awareness, creates posting schedules, curates content that is attuned to your brand image, optimizes content for search engines, designs advertising campaigns, selects posts to boost, runs ads, interacts with followers and so much more.

There are pros and cons of outsourcing your social media, whether you choose to get a freelancer or an agency. The best part about having someone assist you with growing your account is that you can focus your energy on more important things. Some social media managers and agencies charge a premium for their services so go for one that works with your budget and someone who delivers quality.

Pros of hiring a social media manager

#1. You'll save time and avoid the overwhelm and frustration many business owners experience when growing their online presence.

#2. You can leverage the experience and knowledge the social media manager has.

#3. You will finally get someone competent to create a social media strategy for you that aligns with your business goals.

Cons of hiring a social media manager

#1. Hiring a social media can range from $400 to thousands per month, depending on the person. That means you need to have an allocated budget for this.

#2. A social media manager will usually have limited knowledge about your niche or the topic you want to specialize in, so you will need to put in the time to train them to represent you well.

Pros of hiring an agency

#1. They will have the most advanced tools that enhance your ability to quickly grow and monetize your audience.

#2. They come as a complete team, so you will have varying skillsets, all working toward your desired goal.

#3. You will get a higher level of reporting and analytics due to the agency's process.

#4. They bring vast experience and learnings from testing strategies across many clients, leading to rapid strategy innovation and less trial and error.

Cons of hiring an agency

#1. Costs are usually higher.

#2. Response time is often slower, especially when it comes to community management, as the resource is usually not entirely dedicated to one account.

#3. Quality control and sticking to your brand voice and identity can become an issue, so you will need to develop a good process.

#4. The agency might lack specific industry knowledge, which might harm your brand perception and authoritativeness.

#5. Given the high turnover rate of agencies, it's likely that you won't have control over your account because you may be assigned different account managers as people quit and new hires come in. That might create inconsistency and lack of clarity for your Instagram.

Analyze the results

Whether you choose to do it yourself or outsource some help, always remember to keep track of your progress using the right tools.

SECTION 05: MONETIZING YOUR INSTAGRAM

12

MAKING MONEY WITH INSTAGRAM

*I*n this chapter, we will discuss the various ways you can turn raving followers and fans into buying customers so you can continue to grow your brand and reach your financial goals. If you started your Instagram account to make money, here are the easiest ways to start earning an income on Instagram.

Become an Instagram Influencer

You can join the ranks of highly successful and well-paid Instagram influencers by becoming an authoritative figure in your chosen niche. Companies of all sizes will pay you to promote their products and services. You can make as much money as you want and the best part is, you'll be doing something you love. The most important thing is to first build a hyper-engaged audience and earn their trust so you can influence their purchase behavior.

Affiliate marketing

This is the easiest and most common way to make money on Instagram. Affiliate marketing is about promoting someone's product through a link and then receiving a small commission fee for every successful transaction. You can join one of the bigger affiliate opportunities, such as Click-Bank and Amazon Affiliates, or you could get into partnerships with small businesses that have products you believe in. If you're in the personal development or weight loss space, there are hundreds of products you can affiliate from names like Bob Proctor, Tony Robbins, etc.

Sell products and services

These can be physical products and services such as vintage baseball cards or in-house massage services. But that's not all. You can also sell digital products and online services that you create. Think about eBooks, Online courses, Virtual coaching, etc. The best part is with such services you get to keep 100% of the profit.

Become a consultant

As you grow a decent-sized audience, you can start offering social media consulting services or even become an Instagram expert showing others how to grow their accounts fast. I do recommend you always show people or consult based on experiences you've had. So, if you're a trained personal trainer, then yes, you can offer online and offline consultation services. If you've grown your following from zero to 10,000, then yes, provide social media consultations. But always make sure it's something you've gained mastery in first before hanging your hat as a consultant.

Sell your photos

Selling art, photos, and other visual-based elements have become a massive trend on Instagram. If you've got talent and people love your photos, why not give them the option of purchasing either for print or offline use?

I have a friend with 20,000 followers, and all she does is post photos of her sketches. Recently she started offering personalized portraits for a fee, and people have been ordering like crazy. Currently, there's a three-month wait-list or pre-orders. This has taken years to build, but I can assure you, the business is blowing up faster than she can handle. Her product is personalized and very high quality, so she's charging premium prices. Still, people flock to her DM daily with requests. All this to say that it doesn't matter how simple your skill might be. It could be that you take breathtaking nature pics or that you draw the best Manga characters. Instagram is the perfect place to showcase your talents and convert followers into buying customers.

CONCLUSION

You've made it to the end; congratulations on your solid commitment to mastering Instagram marketing. We've covered a lot of ground, and you are all set to survive and thrive in the social media jungle. It may seem like a lot to take in all at once, so please don't read this as entertainment. Instead, I want you to go back and review each chapter and the different action steps suggested, then work on each step before moving to the next.

You now have a better understanding of how Instagram works, how to choose your niche, and identify your ideal audience. I also showed you the basics of brand building, setting up your account the right way, and finding the right hashtags.

Remember that with Instagram, you need to master the fundamentals before getting fancy. So, make sure you improve your pictures, videos, and captions before reaching for the more advanced and fancy solutions to growing engagement.

After years of being on Instagram, I can assure you it will be a continuous hustle, but the rewards are worthwhile. This platform requires constant experimentation and reinvention because it takes a lot to capture users' attention as they scroll through their feed. The fresher and alluring your content is, the easier it will be to grow and scale your account.

The relationships you build with influencers and your followers are the real results you should be aiming for. With that outcome will follow all the rewards you wish to receive, so never take your focus off that objective. And when setbacks catch your off-guard, or things get tough, especially in the first year, don't allow yourself to despair. We've all gone through these hardships.

Although this book guides you through the fundamentals and makes you aware of the blindspots that usually trip people up, it doesn't eliminate all obstacles from your path. The path of entrepreneurship is riddled with hindrances - that's just part of the game. However, you hold in your hand a step-by-step blueprint that will make that journey more bearable and success inevitable if you put in the work.

Now that you know exactly what it takes to turn your Instagram page into a money-making machine and a powerful tool to help you achieve all your goals, it's time to take action and make your dreams a reality.

To your Instagram success

Brandon.

RESOURCES

McFadden, C. (2020, July 2). *A Chronological History of Social Media*. Interesting Engineering. https://interestingengineering.com/a-chronological-history-of-social-media

Patel, N. (2020, January 24). *How To Steal Your Competitor's Social Media Followers*. Neil Patel. https://neilpatel.com/blog/steal-your-competitions-followers/

Chieruzzi, M. (2018, June 26). *Creating, Running, & Managing Instagram Ads: The Step by Step Tutorial*. AdEspresso. https://adespresso.com/guides/instagram-ads/creating-managing-ads/